Avoidant Attachment Recovery

5 Steps to Overcome Fear of Intimacy, Strengthen Connections and Transition from Avoidant to Secure Attachment

Amy Harper

Copyright © 2024 by Amy Harper

All rights reserved.

ISBNs:

- Paperback: 978-1-963174-06-9

- Hardback: 978-1-963174-07-6

The reproduction of any part of this book is prohibited in any form without prior written consent from the publisher or author unless permitted by U.S. copyright law. This publication is crafted to offer precise and authoritative information concerning the covered subject matter. It is distributed with the understanding that neither the author nor the publisher is involved in providing legal, investment, accounting, or other professional services. While the publisher and author have exerted their utmost efforts in composing this book, they make no assurances or guarantees regarding the accuracy or completeness of its contents, explicitly disclaiming any implied warranties of merchantability or fitness for a specific purpose. No warranties can be established or extended by sales representatives or written sales materials. The guidance and strategies contained herein may not be suitable for every situation, and it is advisable to seek professional consultation when necessary. The publisher and author accept no liability for any loss of profit or other commercial damages, encompassing special, incidental, consequential, personal, or other damages.

By reading this document, the reader agrees that under no circumstances is the author responsible for any direct or indirect losses incurred as a result of the use of the information contained within this document, including, but not limited to, errors, omissions, or inaccuracies.

To my family, my steadfast anchors, your love fuels my every endeavor.

Thank you for being my guiding stars.

Preface

Dear Reader,

Thank you for choosing "Avoidant Attachment Recovery." It means a lot to me that you're joining me on this journey.

Throughout my career, I've encountered many individuals battling with walls they've built around themselves, often without realizing it. While I've never personally struggled with avoidant attachment, I've dedicated my professional life to understanding and guiding those who do.

This book is a collection of insights and strategies that have helped people step out of the shadows of avoidance and into the warmth of secure relationships. It's about practical, real-world steps, and it's filled with stories of real progress and hope.

Whether you're just beginning to understand your attachment style or not, this book was written with you in mind. May the pages ahead offer you the tools and confidence to forge stronger connections in your life. I hope you achieve your goals!

Amy Harper

Table of Contents

1. Introduction — 1
   Understanding Attachment Styles

2. Chapter 1 - Step 1 — 11
   The Fundamentals of Self-Discovery & Understanding

3. Chapter 2 - Step 2 — 33
   Emotional Attunement - The Fast-Track to Self-Healing

4. Chapter 3 - Step 3 — 57
   Effective Communication and Embracing Vulnerability

5. Chapter 4 - Step 4 — 83
   Intimacy and Affection

6. Chapter 5 - Step 5 — 101
   Sustainable Growth and Personal Development

7. Conclusion — 127
   The End of the Journey

8. Glossary — 131

9. References — 135

Acknowledgements — 143

Introduction

Understanding Attachment Styles

"There are two philosophies when it comes to getting young children to sleep. There is 'sleep training,' which basically involves putting your kids to bed and listening to them scream all night; or there is 'attachment parenting,' which essentially involves lying down with your kids, cuddling them, and then listening to them scream all night."

Jim Gaffigan

Have you ever felt a confusing mix of wanting connection and pushing people away? It is more common than you may think. Do you see yourself in Amanda? This character's story will deeply resonate with anyone experiencing avoidant attachment.

Amanda is an independent woman in her mid-thirties who came to the big city and made a name for herself with sheer hard work. But now she finds herself alone in the bustling streets of Manhattan and yearns for meaningful connections.

At first glance, Amanda's life appears idyllic. Her bustling café overflows with customers each evening, her boyfriend of two years just proposed, and a vibrant social circle, filled with seemingly close friends, surrounds her.

Yet she isn't the epitome of female empowerment and self-sufficiency as people think. You may look at her to find a lively, confident, and composed businesswoman. But a subtle ache lingers deep within her soul – a longing for intimacy keeps her up at night. Even in the company of her best buddies and would-be husband, she can almost feel a hole in herself.

How did Amanda grow up to be so afraid of intimacy? What makes her a closed book when it comes to expressing emotions? For that, we have to go 20 years in the past. We have to look back at her childhood. As the daughter of an absent father and a negligent mother, Amanda learned to become self-reliant.

She learned how to navigate life's challenges on her own. But this independence came at a price. As a grown-up, she suffers from severe avoidant attachment. As a result, she:

- Is emotionally distant.

- Doesn't let her guard down easily.

- Isn't comfortable seeking help.

- Doesn't like to rely on someone else.

- Is afraid of vulnerability.

- Approach relationships with caution.

- Is apprehensive of intimacy.

- Doesn't express her emotions openly.

Now, she's afraid. Afraid she might push her loved ones away. Afraid that one day, the mask would come off and everyone would see the real Amanda. This fear of losing control manifests in a terrifying possibility - calling off the wedding, severing ties, and running away, repeating the cycle of emotional isolation. What do you think she did next?

Amanda realized she needed to be brave and open up to someone. She sought therapy, talked to a mental health professional, and told her girlfriends about her condition. They were very supportive and told her about a unique new way for people like her to get better.

Unveiling the Secrets of the 5-Step Journey

What did you say? Are you interested in the 5-step program too? Good for you, then! Just like this program worked for Amanda and helped her rediscover her emotional self, it'll do wonders for you, too. Here's a brief overview of the 5 steps and what they cover.

Step One – Self-Discovery and Understanding: Avoidant attachment often works in mysterious ways. It's a pattern that shapes your attachment style over time. Do you avoid intimacy? Do you avoid making long-lasting relationships with other people? All of this might be happening in your subconscious. Well, this phase will be the stepping stone in a long-winded journey in which we'll lay down the much-needed groundwork for change. You'll reflect on your childhood history, previous relationships, and attachment patterns. This stage is for introspection – to look deep into your heart and bury the seed of self-awareness that will bloom into the flower of self-transformation. A few self-assessment exercises will be your tools to make the necessary changes.

Step Two – Emotional Attunement: How much do you understand your emotional landscape? How in touch are you with your emotional side? This stage will help you recognize, validate, and get control of your emotions. Some types of avoidant behaviors stem from these complex feelings that make you bad at emotional regulation. But don't fret; this step will include some fantastic tips to handle your emotions in a healthy way. Is detachment your default mode? Well, this stage will change that, and you'll be more emotionally expressive.

Step Three – Communicating Needs and Embracing Vulnerability: Do you find it difficult to express your needs and desires openly? Does it make you feel bad, abashed, or uncomfortable to open talk about what you need? Because you don't want to be seen as vulnerable, needy, or someone who relies on others? Learn how to embrace vulnerability as your strong suit rather than a weakness. In this stage, we'll tear down the walls that make intimacy an alien concept to you. You will learn practical communication tips so you can be more outspoken about your needs. Find out how to talk to others about your boundaries. It'll help you forge deeper connections with people.

Step Four – Creating Lasting Connections: Now you know how to open up about your feelings. Once people know you're vulnerable, you can move to have a stronger bond with them – a bond of trust, friendship, and mutual reliance. So, this part of the book will cover fantastic tips on nurturing this bond. How do you keep a friendship? How do you make a connection last for months or years? How do you never lose a friend again? Remember, the secret of lasting connections lies not in forging them but in cherishing them. Involve your partner in the process. I'll be there every step of the way to provide unparalleled guidance.

Step Five – Creating Growth and Security: Even newly acquired habits fizzle out and die after a while. How do you avoid relapse? How do you solidify the habits you've picked in the previous four steps? The fifth stage aims to make these new behavior patterns long-lasting and permanent. You will learn to be healthy for good and keep implementing the lessons learned here for the rest of your life. Create an attachment style that stays with you forever. How else are you going to develop lasting and fulfilling relationships? This chapter shows you that overcoming avoidant attachment isn't about following a few processes; it's a lifelong procedure that requires constant effort.

There you have it! You just learned in very brief detail why the 5-step program is helpful to you. How does it help you grow as a person? How does it reveal the hidden side of your personality that you've been suppressing since childhood? In broad strokes, what is the purpose of these five steps?

- Find out what past events make you emotionally detached.

- How to get in touch with your "emotionality" (a pun on sexuality)?

- Tips to make vulnerability your strength and use it to create lasting bonds.

- Nurturing these bonds and making them last for life.

- Growing yourself under the shadow of secure attachment.

The beauty of this program lies in its simplicity and effectiveness. Imagine a powerful roadmap to transformation distilled into just five clear steps, easily remembered and readily implemented. Does this approach resonate with you? Integrating this structured program into your daily routine can become the key to promoting lasting change.

In the next section, you'll learn the reasoning behind these five steps. Find out why a systematic approach always works and helps people easily embrace the lessons of self-recovery.

Why Are We in Love with a Systematic Approach?

There's a fundamental reason why I'm using a systematic approach here. It's a powerful method for change that leads to lasting transformations. Check out these reasons why this approach is ideal for this guide:

- It makes it easier to identify your attachment patterns.

- It gives you a sense of guidance and direction, making the healing process manageable.

- Instead of expecting drastic changes, you will make gradual changes over time, leading to a more sustainable approach to recovery.

- You'll apply self-healing tips chapter by chapter and then apply these skills in the real world. So, don't forget the previous chapter when reading the next one.

- This system makes you reflect on your actions and behaviors. So, you understand how your attachment pattern has affected your romantic life. Self-reflection is the key to permanent healing, right?

- Incremental learning is also great for personal growth. It helps you take control of the healing process. You'll notice an increase in your self-confidence, and soon, it'll be much easier to bring lasting changes.

Just like learning to ride a bike, overcoming avoidant attachment takes practice and a supportive guide. Initially, you might feel a little unsteady and unsure of yourself. But don't worry: I'll be there with you every step of the way, offering support and encouragement. Gradually, as you gain confidence, we can slowly decrease that support. This will allow you to feel more empowered and in control. Soon, you'll be cruising along on your own, navigating your journey with newfound confidence.

A structured program, similar to learning a new skill, equips you with the tools you need to overcome your fear of intimacy and navigate your path to secure attachment.

Do you still think this book doesn't address your needs and concerns? Don't worry; I'll soon explain why this book was written with you in mind. This book is like a novel; you're the main character, my dear reader.

Who am I, and who is This Book for?

Are you wondering if avoidant attachment might be impacting your relationships? Do you want to improve your love life? Be more successful romantically? Reciprocate your partner's feelings for you? Or does your partner sometimes struggle with emotional intimacy, perhaps exhibiting signs of avoidant attachment?

In all cases, this is the perfect book for you. Does keeping your partner at arm's length sound familiar? Avoidant attachment could be the reason. Learn how to create a closer bond.

My name is Amy Harper, and I am your guide and companion throughout this journey of healing and recovery. I'm here to support you on your journey to overcome avoidant attachment. Please think of me as your guide and cheerleader, helping you conquer those intimacy fears and build the relationships you deserve.

Throughout my career as a counselor, I've encountered many individuals with a variety of behavioral challenges. Among them, I've observed a significant number who experience avoidant attachment. In fact, research suggests it affects roughly 30% of the global population, which highlights its prevalence. My deep understanding of this condition has led me to write this book.

In this book, Avoidant Attachment Recovery, I'll discuss this condition in detail. So, don't lose hope; your quest toward secure attachment is only a few pages away. But first, you have to keep a few principles in mind to speed up the healing process.

Setting the Tone - A Journey of Change

You may wonder how this book will help you become a changed person. Well, let's set the tone for the whole book here in this small section. When you're reading this book, keep these three principles in your mind – like a charm that'll help you heal faster:

1. You'll overcome avoidant attachment one day; we'll keep this hope alive.

2. Let healing come from a place of empathy, understanding, and compassion.

3. This book is your judgment-free zone for exploring your emotions. Let your guard down and discover a path to greater intimacy.

Never forget that the seedling of healing and growth lies deep within your heart. You are in control and possess the power to change yourself. With little effort, you can push that seed to grow into a small plant of self-realization that will soon bloom into a huge plant of permanent healing. Positive changes lie ahead, and this book is the road to recovery. You are the driver, so have faith in your skills. I believe you can do it. Do you?

This journey is a team effort. While this book offers valuable tools, your active participation unlocks its full potential.

Read the following section carefully and find the key that makes this book work.

What do I Want from You?

If you want to make this healing process work, cooperate with me. Here's what I want you to do while reading this guide:

- Open yourself up to the contents of this book. The more actively you participate, the greater the rewards.

- Engage emotionally with the tips mentioned here.

- Approach each chapter with an open mind and the desire to change.

- Always be prepared to reflect on what you've read, grow with it, and make healing part of your daily routine.

Let's embark on this incredible journey of healing and self-discovery. Whether you want to revitalize your romantic life or get back the one who got away, this guide will help you through and through. From Chapter 1, the healing process begins!

Chapter 1 - Step 1

The Fundamentals of Self-Discovery & Understanding

> "I think self-discovery is the greatest achievement in life because once you discover yourself and accept who you are, you can fulfill your true potential and be happy."
>
> Marco Pierre White

I see that you're reading Chapter 1 now. The bravest thing a person could do is to step on the road of self-discovery. That's when your transformation begins, and you slowly become a better person. It isn't easy to confront your fears and vulnerabilities head-on or even acknowledge that they exist. It takes courage to say, "I have this flaw and need help."

As your fingers keep turning these pages and your eyes glance upon these words, you shouldn't forget that you're not alone in this journey. Many have walked this path before and will do after you. Surveys show that over 14% of kids in America have an avoidant attachment (Ocklenburg, 2023). These kids will likely grow up to walk the path you're walking right now.

So, are you willing to explore your attachment style? Do you wish to bring everlasting changes in your life? I should warn you that the journey you're about to undertake isn't that easy. No, sir! You may have to face ugly truths about yourself, face the aspects of your personality you've always avoided, and shatter the beliefs that affected your romantic life. But remember this: every step you take will bring you closer to self-awareness and a more fulfilling life.

You'll learn some crucial answers on this quest, such as:

- What are the signs of avoidant attachment?

- How does it affect your relationships?

- How do you embrace a secure attachment style?

So, embrace this journey with an open heart and mind. Don't forget our shared goal is not perfection but progress. So, let's make this progress together, my friend!

Avoidant Attachment - Recognizing the Telltale Signs

I've been providing counseling to people with behavior issues. Many of my clients struggle with avoidant attachment and similar conditions. One of my clients was Jessica, a 25-year-old schoolteacher married to her high school sweetheart. Her story can help you recognize the telltale signs of avoidant attachment.

Now, Jessica wasn't an introvert; she liked to hang around with friends and partying with them. At her job (I knew her because she taught one of my kids), she was every kid's favorite teacher. But there was still something missing in her life.

Sometimes, she used to choose to stay at home and do nothing. She told me she sometimes spent hours watching movies on her tablet and didn't respond to her friends. They wanted to go shopping – and Jessica loved shopping – but she used to say no. Or even left her best friend on read without even bothering to respond.

Even her husband had to suffer because of her emotionally distant attitude; he wanted to spend time with her, but she didn't reciprocate the same warmth and love. Even when they were out – like watching a movie or having a double date with mutual friends – she was always miles away in her own thoughts. In any social gathering, she was the least talkative person.

And Jessica was aware of all that. She just didn't know how to start connecting with people and stop ghosting her childhood friends. Even her work productivity began to decline due to her condition. She stopped showing up for team-building exercises or helping new teachers adjust to the environment. "I am afraid to rely on others, and I also don't want anyone else counting on me."

Then Jessica shared the thing she was terrified of the most. She was afraid that if she kept pushing people away, she might end up ending things with her husband, the man whom she very much loved. It was a thought that kept her awake at night, but she didn't know what she could do about it.

After reading Jessica's story, you can see interesting parallels. You want to behave like her in real life, don't you? Honestly answer these simple questions:

- Do you choose to be alone even if you want to be with friends?
- Do you cut your friends off and struggle to respond to them?
- Do you refuse to socialize with your coworkers?
- Do you try to do things by yourself all the time?

- Do you pull away when your partner wants to be close to you?

As the saying goes (or my kids made it up and told it to me), "Name the beast to tame the beast." Realizing your flaws and recognizing your symptoms are the very first stepping stones toward healing. If you wish to start your journey toward the secure shores of secure attachment, evaluate your attachment pattern.

Self-Assessment - How Well Do You Know Your Attachment Style?

Let's start with a brief session of self-assessment. We must ensure you understand your current attachment style and avoidant tendencies very well.

Below, you'll find a list of the key avoidant tendencies often exhibited by avoidantly attached people. Please read each question carefully and then honestly assess your current level of proficiency on a scale of 1 to 5. The self-assessment in this book is designed for self-reflection and isn't an official diagnosis. It's a helpful way to gauge your tendency for avoidant behaviors, but it's important to consult with a professional for a proper evaluation and advice.

- "1" means a strong "Yes" (indicating Strong Avoidance).
- "2" means a mild "Yes" (indicating Mild Avoidance).
- "3" means neutrality, i.e., neither "Yes" nor "No."
- "4" means a mild "No" (indicating Mild Security).
- "5" means a strong "No" (indicating Strong Security).

1- Do you feel emotionally distant from your partner, family, and friends?

☐1 ☐2 ☐3 ☐4 ☐5

2- Do you always try to do things on your own and don't like accepting help?

☐1 ☐2 ☐3 ☐4 ☐5

3- Do you approach new relationships with caution and are suspicious of men/women seeking your companionship?

☐1 ☐2 ☐3 ☐4 ☐5

4- Does intimacy seem like a scary concept to you? Does it make you uncomfortable or wear you down?

☐1 ☐2 ☐3 ☐4 ☐5

5- Does self-expression make you embarrassed? Do you not like showing emotions?

☐1 ☐2 ☐3 ☐4 ☐5

6- Are you the kind of person who doesn't want to rely on others and doesn't want others to rely on you?

☐1 ☐2 ☐3 ☐4 ☐5

7- Is it hard for you to respond to your friends, leading to unread chats and unseen messages?

☐1 ☐2 ☐3 ☐4 ☐5

8- Is it hard for you to socialize with your coworkers since you don't want to be too attached to them?

☐1 ☐2 ☐3 ☐4 ☐5

9- Do you choose to be a loner despite your strong desire for intimacy and hanging out with friends?

☐1 ☐2 ☐3 ☐4 ☐5

10- Does it make you mad when people try to be close to you, and you think they are being too clingy?

☐1 ☐2 ☐3 ☐4 ☐5

11- Do you sometimes think you're not worthy of your partner's love or that he/she deserves someone better?

☐1 ☐2 ☐3 ☐4 ☐5

12- Does criticism make you too depressed? It makes you think low of yourself?

☐1 ☐2 ☐3 ☐4 ☐5

13- Do you try to keep a poker face (show-no-emotion face) when dealing with tough times?

☐1 ☐2 ☐3 ☐4 ☐5

14- Do you refuse to give or take emotional support? Do you expect others to be just as emotionally distant as you are?

☐1 ☐2 ☐3 ☐4 ☐5

15- Do you spend or want to spend most of your time alone? Do you describe yourself as a loner?

☐1 ☐2 ☐3 ☐4 ☐5

16- Do you think you're not 100% invested in your current relationship? Do you keep suspecting, "Something will go wrong in this relationship?"

☐1   ☐2   ☐3   ☐4   ☐5

17- Are you always suspicious of your partner? Do you think they might cheat on you, dump you, or disappoint you some other way?

☐1   ☐2   ☐3   ☐4   ☐5

18- Do you stay away from intimacy because you are afraid of being rejected by your partner?

☐1   ☐2   ☐3   ☐4   ☐5

19- Are you always the one to prematurely end the relationship?

☐1   ☐2   ☐3   ☐4   ☐5

20- Are you commitment-shy? Are you afraid to make a commitment or invest in a relationship?

☐1   ☐2   ☐3   ☐4   ☐5

21- Are you bad at reading emotions? Do you have a hard time recognizing people's emotions or understanding how they feel?

☐1   ☐2   ☐3   ☐4   ☐5

22- Do you fantasize about a relationship after it ends? Do you muse over your exes?

☐1   ☐2   ☐3   ☐4   ☐5

23- Do you deliberately or accidentally sabotage your own relationship?

☐1   ☐2   ☐3   ☐4   ☐5

24- Do you believe intimacy is the same as vulnerability?

☐1   ☐2   ☐3   ☐4   ☐5

25- Do you try to get out of a relationship when it gets more serious?

☐1   ☐2   ☐3   ☐4   ☐5

26- Are you unwilling to open up to your partner about your personal life?

☐1   ☐2   ☐3   ☐4   ☐5

27- Do you avoid difficult conversations and try to stay miles away from hard-to-handle topics?

☐1   ☐2   ☐3   ☐4   ☐5

28- Do you get visibly disturbed when your partner brings up delicate topics?

☐1   ☐2   ☐3   ☐4   ☐5

29- Do you feel like you always have to be perfect and give your 100% to everything?

☐1   ☐2   ☐3   ☐4   ☐5

30- Does sharing too much information embarrass you? Does it make you feel naked and wounded?

☐1   ☐2   ☐3   ☐4   ☐5

31- Do you ruminate over bygone events and bad experiences of the past?

☐1   ☐2   ☐3   ☐4   ☐5

32- Do you easily get offended when someone judges or condemns you?

☐1   ☐2   ☐3   ☐4   ☐5

33- Do you keep changing sexual partners?

☐1   ☐2   ☐3   ☐4   ☐5

34- Do you prefer to engage sexually with someone you're not romantically attached to?

☐1   ☐2   ☐3   ☐4   ☐5

35- Do you think negatively of people who are securely attached to their partners?

☐1   ☐2   ☐3   ☐4   ☐5

36- Are you estranged from your parents, siblings, or children?

☐1   ☐2   ☐3   ☐4   ☐5

37- Do you blame yourself for your avoidant tendencies?

☐1   ☐2   ☐3   ☐4   ☐5

38- Do you think therapy or counseling isn't something for you?

☐1   ☐2   ☐3   ☐4   ☐5

39- Do you prefer being with yourself over shared activities with your partner?

☐1   ☐2   ☐3   ☐4   ☐5

40- Do you end friendships or refrain from making new ones due to your fear of intimacy?

☐1   ☐2   ☐3   ☐4   ☐5

Please take a moment to reflect on your responses and consider areas where you may want to focus your efforts for improvement. I encourage you to read the book and try out what you will learn in your own life. Then come back and re-do this assessment to see where you improved and where you still need to focus on.

It's Ancient History - Tracing the Roots of Avoidance

How do we trace the roots of avoidant attachment? For that, we've got to plunge deep into the memory lane and peek into our childhood. Consider Amanda's example and how a childhood filled with unrealized wants and unmet desires made her the woman she later became.

Can you recall anything from your past that made you the way you are now? Remember, there's no judgment here. We're merely doing this exercise to understand what makes you "you."

Some studies have pointed out that three major factors are responsible for avoidant attachment in adults (Wardecker et al., 2020), namely:

1. Your personality traits (e.g., are you an introvert or extrovert?).

2. Significant life events (e.g., a sick sibling getting all the attention from parents).

3. Cultural influences (e.g., do you come from a culture where boys are preferred by parents and girls get the crumbs?).

Research also shows that a person's experience with their earliest caregivers influences her attachment style (Riggio et al., 2020). In most cases, these caregivers were your parents. You may develop avoidant attachment if your parents:

- Criticized you too much when you were a kid.

- Didn't look after your medical needs if you were sick.

- Didn't feed you enough to worry about your well-being.

- Made fun of you or didn't pay you enough attention.

- Weren't there for you when you were stressed out.

Do you remember the very first quote? Jim Gaffigan says that parents can either put their kids to bed and listen to them scream all night or lie in bed with them and then listen to them scream. You can see that the second approach is obviously excellent parenting. But it's the first approach that sows the oats of avoidant tendencies in kids.

We have to look into the type of care you received in your childhood. So, I need you to go back in the past and look at various stages of your life – childhood, teenage years, and adulthood. What do you see?

Do you see a pattern? A pattern of neglect, contempt, and emotional unavailability? Recognize these patterns, and you're golden!

Check out these questions, and they might help you remember something from your past – a memory you were keeping hidden deep inside:

- Did your parents save you from bullies at school?

- Did your parents or caregivers attend parent-teacher meetings?

- Were your caregivers there for you when you needed them the most?

- Were you and your siblings equally loved and valued?

- Did your caregivers spend time with you after coming back from work?

- Did any of your caregivers have a substance use disorder?

- Did your parents have a divorce? If yes, then how did it affect you?

The kind of care and treatment you received as a kid may have evolved you into a more emotionally distant person. Your childhood experiences are impacting your love life and reshaping your relationship dynamics. Hopefully, you can see the constituents of your present-day avoidant tendencies. Now, we can work toward progress and healing.

The key idea here is understanding what causes avoidant attachment and how it impacts your overall well-being. Only then we'll be able to do something about it. For now, here's what I recommend you do:

- How do you process these feelings about your childhood? Write them down. Pick journaling as a hobby. Keep a diary where you write about how the neglect you've been subjected to in the past keeps haunting you even today.

- It'll help you find a very prominent link between your childhood experiences and current behavior patterns. You'll realize how those memories are responsible for your current avoidant tendencies.

- Most importantly, don't blame your caregivers. Let sleeping dogs lie. Let bygones be bygones. This exercise is only meant to help you understand your trauma. So, learn to forgive but not forget.

Don't worry, dear reader. Soon, we'll explore how much your upbringing impacts your attachment style. It'll help you begin a journey of healing.

Avoidant attachment can leave you feeling isolated, longing for connection, yet hesitant to pursue it. But fear not! This book will be your guiding light, helping you navigate the challenges and illuminate a path to secure attachment. Next, let's explore some common behavior patterns associated with this condition.

Avoidance Decoded - Recognizing Behavior Patterns

You can now quickly recognize the telltale behavior patterns associated with avoidant attachment. In simple words, this is what avoidant attachment looks like (Lampe et al., 2018):

- You yearn for intimacy.
- But you also fear rejection.
- You don't trust your partner fully.

Does it ring a bell? Do you often display a sense of emotional detachment? Are you afraid of connecting with people intimately? Do you prefer to keep to yourself most of the time? It suggests you may have an avoidant attachment style (Wardecker et al., 2020).

If you still need more help recognizing the behavior patterns of avoidance, we can get help from a well-known character – a person we all love.

Do You Remember Chandler Bing from Friends?

Who doesn't remember Chandler's humor and sarcasm? But have you ever noticed how he shows clear signs of avoidant tendencies? The neglect he faced as a kid from his parents made him fearful of commitment to such an extent that he sabotaged his relationships to avoid getting too close to his girlfriends.

He leans on sarcasm to deflect serious conversations, especially when the topic touches his emotions. And what else? He's married to someone even more avoidant than him.

Yes, Monica Geller is another classic example of avoidant tendencies that stem from past trauma. All Friends fans know how Monica always lived in Ross's shadow, who was preferred by her parents for being a "medical marvel," while Monica stayed under heavy scrutiny by a picky mother. So, she develops a protective shell around herself, engages in obsessive-compulsive behavior, and can be quite controlling of herself.

These two examples will help you understand the telltale signs of avoidant tendencies. If you still have trouble determining these very obvious behavior patterns, then I suggest you check these everyday examples and see if they fit you:

- Try to recall all the relationships you've had in the past. Do you have a history of always being the one who ends a relationship? How many romantic partners have you pushed away by breaking up with them?

- Are you commitment-shy? Suppose your partner proposes to go on a vacation or plans a quick weekend getaway. But you never show any interest in doing these activities with them even though you love spending time with your partner?

- Do you think you're worthy of love? Suppose your partner tries to make big gestures of love – as they do in movies, such as hiring-a-Mariachi-band-to-serenade-you kind of gestures – and it makes you uncomfortable.

- Have you ever sabotaged a relationship like Chandler? Nitpicking a relationship is yet another example of avoidant attachment.

- Do you have trouble reading emotions? A study shows that avoidant individuals aren't very good at reading emotions and can't determine why their partner is mad at them (Schumann et al., 2019).

- Do you fantasize about someone who got away? Suppose a past boyfriend seems to you like an ideal partner now. Since you've been obsessed with that relationship for the past, you're emotionally unavailable to your current partner.

- What words do you use when talking to your partner? Suppose your partner asks you, "Where do you see this relationship going?" And then you start talking about freedom, independence, and self-reliance. If your philosophy is "I'm all I've got," it might be a problem.

- We've already talked about how avoidant individuals don't trust anyone and are always suspicious of their romantic partners. Do you think your partner is always trying to take advantage of you or take away your freedom? This paranoia may be a sign of avoidant attachment.

- Has your partner ever told you that you send them mixed messages? Showering them with love one day and then pushing them away? Do you tell your partner you want to spend more time with them, but then you cram your schedule with other tasks? Yes, these mixed messages aren't healthy at all.

- Do you always have an exit strategy to weasel out of social obligations or escape a social gathering? Especially when you had promised your boyfriend that you would show up for that thing?

These are ten telltale signs of avoidant attachment in people. Review these behavior patterns and try to see parallels in your own behavior or your loved one's behavior. Wait a second. Pick up your pen and start writing any instances where your avoidant tendencies appeared. Journaling – as mentioned earlier – improves self-understanding. So, you can easily change your behavior and progress toward secure attachment.

Don't forget that avoidant attachment also impacts your mental health. It leads to stress, anxiety, depression, and social withdrawal (Momeni et al., 2022). Moreover, keep in mind that your partner also suffers with you. When you don't connect with your partner emotionally, they feel:

- Irritated
- Insecure
- Disgruntled

If you value your partner and want to continue your romantic journey successfully, follow the healing exercises mentioned in this book.

I'll introduce some of these exercises in the next section. That's how you can begin your journey toward healing and romantic bliss.

Healing Old Wounds - How to Reprocess Trauma?

As Marco Pierre White beautifully puts it, the train bound to happiness leaves the station of self-discovery. You can't move forward without burying the skeletons in your closet. Unless you heal old wounds, new ones will keep appearing. That's why it's very, very important to reprocess your trauma to start all over.

Do you know how bad unresolved trauma can be? Research says that unresolved trauma can be hereditary; it'll pass from mothers to kids, affecting entire generations (Iyengar et al., 2014). As a result, kids are born with insecure attachments already coded in their genes. You can see how past trauma – even if it goes back to your ancestors – can affect your love life in the 21st century (and, if not addressed promptly, your grandkids' lives in the 22nd century!). So, here's what you have to do (Karantzas et al., 2023):

- Embrace your vulnerability and acknowledge there are demons in your past.

- Engage in self-awareness training to become more in tune with your true self.

- Question your dysfunctional beliefs and challenge your long-held notions about romantic relationships.

Don't forget that your avoidant behaviors likely stem from your childhood trauma. In fact, your avoidant tendencies are a natural response to the pain you suffered in the past. It is like Chandler's sarcasm or Monica's OCD – these are defense mechanisms that allow your brain to deal with trauma while keeping you functional in everyday life. They will:

- Change your entire thought process.

- Make it difficult to trust other people.

- Reinforce your avoidant tendencies.

- Leave your isolated, frustrated, and angry inside.

- Make you feel "dead inside" or emotionally distant from others.

As a result, you will feel defensive whenever your partner even mildly taunts you. Their words or actions may startle you. You will feel disconnected from them and less excited to engage in intimate or sexual activities with them. What's worse – in some cases – you may even begin questioning, "Do I even love them anymore?"

That's why trauma-induced avoidant attachment leads to conflicts in your relationship. A person with avoidant tendencies will feel alienated from her lover. It seems okay to go deeper into the concept of trauma. I promise I won't bore you with medical details. I will keep it simple and digestible.

What Is Trauma, and What Causes It?

Don't get confused by the word "trauma" being used in different medical fields. We are talking about psychological trauma, a stressful event that you lack the emotions to deal with. This event will shatter your sense of security, make you feel helpless in the world, and overwhelm your ability to cope (Wang et al., 2023). It leads to the resurfacing of past experiences that can impact your daily routines.

From being in a war zone and facing police brutality to suffering from childhood abuse and being in a traffic accident – trauma has many sources:

- Domestic abuse.
- Sexual violence.
- Harassment and bullying.
- Abandonment and neglect.
- Being kidnapped.
- Caught in the middle of a natural disaster.

- Experiencing complications during childbirth.

But don't think of your trauma as an insurmountable monster, a dragon nobody can slay. Trauma can be defeated. Check out these fantastic evidence-based techniques to deal with your trauma. Overcoming your trauma will also help you take back control of your romantic life and reverse the effects of avoidant attachment.

- **Journaling:** Once, my husband introduced me to a friend of his, a veteran who was struggling with PTSD. I asked him how he managed to overcome this serious condition. He smiled and showed me a small notebook he carried everywhere. It was his "trauma journal," where he wrote his thoughts and feelings. Research has shown that expressive writing is a great way to cope with your trauma and reduce the intensity of its symptoms (Tull et al., 2020).

- **Guided Visualization:** I call it guided visualization, but you may have heard of it as guided imagery. A therapist will help shift your thoughts toward peaceful scenes or events. This meditative technique is fantastic for folks dealing with trauma. It'll keep you in the present and help you regain mental peace.

- **Controlled Exposure:** Remember how they say to face your fears? Well, that's what therapists do in this practice. You're brought face to face with the things you fear in a controlled environment. It's like building up a tolerance, similar to that ancient king who supposedly ingested small doses of poison to become immune. We can gradually expose ourselves to challenging situations safely to build resilience. In a safe space, you learn to be strong, face your fears, and overpower them. It's a great way to beat your trauma and slowly become resistant to its harmful effects.

Traumatic memories can have a lot of power over you. But you can't let them dictate your romantic relationships, can you? Use these techniques to manage the effects of trauma and build healthy, fulfilling partnerships. Most importantly – be compassionate to yourself. Don't give yourself a tough time. What would you do if your best bud has trauma and asks for your help in his healing journey? Approach your trauma with the same kindness you would offer that friend.

Don't let your attachment style dictate your love life. It's time to take back control and start the process of healing. We're making progress here, dear reader. Now, let's move on to the next phase of our quest for recovery.

Key Takeaways

- Recognize the telltale signs of avoidant tendencies, such as obsessing over "me time," hating being touched, or thinking your partner is too clingy.

- The roots of avoidance may lie in childhood, e.g., your caregivers criticized, mocked, insulted, or neglected you excessively.

- If you have unprocessed and traumatic feelings about your childhood, they can explain your avoidant behavior as an adult.

- Some signs of avoidant attachment are being commitment-shy, bad at reading emotions and being the first to end relationships.

- Reprocess your trauma with techniques like guided visualization and controlled exposure to overcome avoidant tendencies.

Sneak Peak: What's in Chapter 2?

Congratulations – you've completed the preliminary phase of the quest. What lies ahead? This is what awaits you in the next chapter:

- What is emotional attunement?

- Tips to bolster your emotional awareness.

- Mindful and its role in honing your emotional well-being.

- How do you regulate your emotions and keep them stable?

- Tackling the reasons why you are afraid of intimacy.

This exciting journey into the depths of avoidant attachment will not stop anytime soon. We've just covered the first step of the journey. Four more pit stops are up ahead in our adventure.

Chapter 2 - Step 2

Emotional Attunement - The Fast-Track to Self-Healing

"Just like children, emotions heal when they are heard and validated."

Jill Bolte Taylor

Welcome to the second phase of your journey. The hardest part of the quest is over as you've pinpointed the past trauma responsible for your avoidant tendencies. In this chapter, you'll learn how to start the healing process and open up to people emotionally.

Throughout this book, you'll realize that true strength comes from opening up to others. You become weak when you refuse to entertain other people's emotions. Sadly for our girl Mina, she learned this lesson the hard way.

As the daughter of neglectful parents who were preoccupied with their own problems, Mina learned to be self-sufficient. As a result, she has avoidant tendencies now. She is unwilling and unable to recognize other people's emotions.

Her worst nightmare is people trying to open up to her. When someone – a coworker or a seemingly lovely guy at a bar – tries to connect with her emotionally, she withdraws. She practically screams at these people in their mind, saying: "Get away from me. Don't you see I'm the wrong person to have a heart-to-heart with?"

She always keeps her distance from people, whether they're close friends or not, afraid to get too close.

It all changes when she meets the girl of her dreams. Her partner gently encourages her to regulate her emotions and be mindful of other people's feelings. With time, our sweet Mina learns to trust people and practice emotional attunement. She actively listens to what a person has to say – especially if that person is her girlfriend – and expresses her own feelings openly. Mina says the best lesson she ever learned was never to trivialize other people's emotions.

Emotions can be damaged and hurt badly when they are trivialized and ignored. But the best way to heal emotions is to hear them, validate them, and nurture them in a supportive environment.

That's the power of emotional attunement. It did miracles for Mina and her soon-to-be wife. It can do magic for your romantic life as well.

Emotional Attunement and Your Attachment Style

Let's get to the brass tacks. What on God's green Earth is emotional attunement? What does it have to do with your attachment style and romantic setbacks? In simple terms, it means to do the following:

- Understand your partner's feelings.

- Recognize the way they feel about you.

- Respect their emotions and complaints.

- Validate their experiences with you.

- Fully engage with their emotional state.

Remember when we learned about avoidant individuals in Chapter 1? They are bad at reading people's emotions, so emotional attunement is Greek to them. Reading people's emotions can also be challenging because not everyone opens up about their feelings via spoken words. No, sir! You also have to read gestures, facial cues, and body language to understand what your partner is going through.

However, once you get in tune with your significant other's emotional state, it will boost your relationship. Emotional attunement will make your partner feel (Webb et al., 2023):

- Seen

- Heard

- Known

- Accepted

- Acknowledged

The best way to tell your partner, "I care about you and love you," is to recognize, accept, and validate their emotions. You may wonder how it's done. To be honest, it's not that hard. You just have to sit down and listen to your partner.

I admire what John M. Gottman writes about emotional attunement. Do read his book The Science of Trust if you can. He suggests you and your partner sit down for an hour to process your negative emotions and build trust in each other. Here's how it is done:

- Spend an hour every week talking about your relationship.

- Take turns as speaker and listener.

- Write down your thoughts when the other person is speaking.

- Talk about what's going right in your relationship.

- Mention 5 to 10 things you like about your partner.

- Discuss if you feel there's something you'd like to change in this relationship.

- Don't judge, blame, or criticize your partner.

- State your feelings in a neutral way.

- Instead of "you" statements, use "I" statements.

- Validate your partner's feelings and emotions.

Did you see what happened here? This brief exercise helped you get in touch with not just your partner's emotions but also your own. This is the fantastic thing about emotional attunement, i.e., it makes you self-aware. A person who is in touch with their emotions and recognizes other people's feelings in a snap is on the fast track to secure attachment.

Here's how avoidant and secure attachment styles differ when it comes to emotional attunement:

- **Secure Attachment:** These people are open to emotional experiences.

- **Avoidant Attachment:** As illustrated in Mina's example, these people dislike emotional openness and disconnect from emotions as a defense mechanism.

As a result, your interpersonal skills suffer. So:

- You don't communicate well.
- You don't do well with conflicts.
- You can't be a team with your partner.

For example, if your partner is having a bad day, what will you do? Will you listen to their complaints about their unproductive day? Will you make them feel heard? Will you offer a word of sympathy, a shoulder to cry on?

In avoidant attachment, you may end up doing nothing, shutting yourself in a shell of emotional disconnection. Just imagine how your partner will feel if you are unwilling to even indulge in their experiences.

So, do the Gottman exercise to hone your emotional attunement skills.

Next, we'll check excellent exercises to make you more emotionally aware. That's how you can overcome your avoidant tendencies by the end of this book.

Six Ways to Enhance Emotional Awareness

How well do you understand your emotions? Can you easily make sense of your thoughts and innermost feelings? Developing emotional awareness is a crucial step on the journey to secure attachment.

Studies show that women—especially mothers—can move faster toward full recovery if they perform emotional awareness exercises (Monti et al., 2014). But how do you become more emotionally aware?

Harnessing the hidden powers of emotional awareness isn't tricky. When you're upset, do you take time to figure out what you're actually feeling? Do you try to work out why you feel suspicious of your partner? Asking simple questions is the proper way to connect with your emotional side.

These detailed and practical exercises will help you tune into your emotional states and be more wary of your inner feelings:

1: Emotional Check-ins

Check-in with your emotions at least once a day. Ask yourself, "How am I doing? What do I feel?" Be your own mini-therapist and maintain a record of your emotions. Here's what you should do:

- Get a notebook app or pick your journal.
- Record your emotions every night before sleeping.
- Write about the intensity of these emotions and what caused them.
- Keep reviewing this diary to determine the common triggers of your anxiety.

There you go! Now you know what disturbs your emotional peace so that you can stay away from these triggers.

2: Full-Body Scanning

Some emotions aren't that easily noticeable. You may have to dig deeper into your emotional state via a process called full-body scanning. This meditative exercise helps redirect your attention to your body.

As a result, you'll see your anxiety and stress melting away (Kogan et al., 2021). I love doing this exercise with the family-favorite golden retriever sitting by my side. Here's how it's done:

- Set in a meditative yoga pose.

- Scan your body from head to toe.

- Do you notice any physical sensations?

- Do you notice any emotional cues when scanning your body parts?

You're now more aware of your bodily sensations and feelings.

3: Label Your Emotions

Emotions are like people; once you know their names, they're easier to recognize. That's why you should label your emotions as they arise to acknowledge. It's a fantastic way to reduce the intensity of negative emotions and cope with them effectively.

Get on a first-name basis with your emotions; you'll find them easy to control. Do keep these tips in mind when performing this exercise, however:

- Don't just name your emotions "good," "bad," "happy," "angry," or "sad."

- Identify the specific nature of your emotions. How exactly do they make you feel?

- Give them names like "envy," "suspicion," "kindness," "jealousy," "calmness," and "admiration."

4: The Five Whys of Emotions

In this exercise, you ask yourself a single question "Why?" five times. It helps you get to the root cause of your emotional distress. Learn the deeper reasons why you feel the way you do. Explore your anxiety layer by layer to discover the underlying causes (Taibbi, 2014).

The roots of the "Five Whys" technique lie in a curious concept labeled as "emotional granularity," or the ability to experience your emotions in a particular manner (Tan et al., 2022). Granularity helps you tell different emotions apart as well as label the more discrete ones. As you ask yourself the question "Why?" several times, you can understand your emotional experiences better and be "granular" in this understanding.

Consider the example of a person suspicious of her partner all the time. She will ask herself five times "Why?"

- Why am I suspicious? Because I think my partner wants to usurp my freedom.

- Why does that make me afraid? Because I value my freedom above all.

- Why do I value it so much? Because I'm afraid to rely on others.

- Why am I afraid? Because I don't trust people easily.

- Why don't I trust people? Because I have been betrayed before.

5: Emotion Pairing

Emotional pairing is a simple technique where you deliberately connect challenging emotions to positive ones. The goal is to balance out tough feelings by focusing on a positive counterpart. You may have heard there are 34,000 emotions for humans to experience. Sounds kind of overwhelming, right? Don't worry; psychologist Robert Plutchik says there are merely eight basic emotions, namely (Semeraro et al., 2021):

- Joy
- Fear
- Trust
- Anger
- Disgust
- Sadness
- Surprise
- Anticipation

So, here's what you should do: Identify the emotions that are difficult for you to handle and match them with positive emotions that can help balance your mood. For instance, if anger is something you struggle with, try pairing it with confidence to counteract its effects. This way, you won't feel overwhelmed by negative emotions. This exercise is also great for improving emotional regulation.

6: Emotion Pacing

Remember controlled exposure? This one's similar to that exercise. In this highly effective routine, you slowly bring yourself face to face with the emotions you usually avoid. But you do this in a controlled environment, in your safe space.

Use guided visualization to approach these undesirable emotions little by little. It'll help you get familiar with experiencing them and, ultimately, defeating them.

It is facing your fears all over again, but this time, you're doing it on your own.

Use these simple tools in your everyday life. Whether you're communicating with your partner, tackling friendships, or dealing with coworkers – these exercises will always come in handy. Self-awareness will lead to better progress in our joint efforts to alter your attachment style.

Keep practicing until you master the subtle art of self-awareness. You may wonder what's next in this quest. In the next section, we'll focus on emotional regulation and share a step-by-step guide to keep your emotions in check. So, don't let your feelings get the best of you.

Emotional Regulation - The Key to Secure Attachment

Do you want to manage your intense emotions and reactionary behaviors? It is the best way to understand what emotional regulation is. What does it entail? How does a person stabilize emotions?

Trust me; emotional regulation is one of the main building blocks of secure attachment. People who are in control of their emotional side can form healthy, long-lasting romantic connections.

So, let's check out some tips to tame your emotions.

What is Emotional Regulation?

Have you ever felt a sudden surge of rage and didn't know how to suppress it? Have you said very insensitive things to your partner and later regretted it? You may often find yourself in a cataclysm of conflicting emotions – rage filled with uncertainty, suspicion with denial – and you don't know how to get over these weird feelings.

Emotional regulation is the ability to control and influence your emotions. It helps you make sense of the following dilemmas (Kozubal et al., 2023):

- What kind of emotions will you have?

- When and where will you experience these emotions?

- How will you experience these emotions and express them?

Learning emotional regulation will prevent embarrassment, angry outbursts in public, grieving conflicts with your partner, and the constant feeling of detachment from your lover. Here are a few tips – presented in the form of interrelated questions – to help you regulate your emotions:

- What are your emotional or psychological triggers?

- What triggers strong emotional responses in you?

- Are there people, events, or situations that trigger your emotional outbursts?

- In what situations do you normally stay emotionally stable?

- Which triggers are easy to ignore, and which ones are hard to let go of?

But these simple suggestions are like the tip of the iceberg. We'll soon see more fantastic tips on emotional regulation. So, stay tuned, and keep reading. You've made progress in the past few pages. Don't let the success train get off track.

How to Regulate Your Emotions Like a Boss

Don't forget that the purpose of emotional regulation is not to suppress your emotions. Having emotions is normal – they are a natural reaction to different life events. We only need emotional regulation to:

- Understand our emotions.

- Trace what causes them.

- Respond to them appropriately.

Here are four tried-and-trusted exercises to help regulate your emotions:

1. **Breathing Exercises:** I always recommend breathing exercises to my clients. They're a fantastic way to release tension and bring greater balance to your emotional state. You can do them by controlling your breathing, i.e., inhale for 4 seconds, hold it for 7, and exhale for 8. Whenever you feel like your stress is beyond your control, use this exercise to be in charge of your emotional self.

2. **Cognitive Reframing:** If you ever find yourself wallowing in the bottomless pit of self-blame and low self-esteem, use this method to shift your negative thoughts and replace them with positive ideas (Mueser et al., 2015). Use phrases, mantras, and positive sentences to shift your perspective. Say things like "I'm doing great," "I'm worthy of love,""Remember why I started this journey," and others to alter your negative mindset.

3. **Muscle Relaxation:** Do you know that anxiety and stress man-

ifest as physical tension in your muscles? Progressive Muscle Relaxation (PMR) can cure this very troublesome issue by tensing and releasing each muscle group. The idea is that a relaxed body isn't easily stressed out. So, get massage therapy to calm your mind and make it immune to the effects of emotional upheavals.

4. **Timeouts:** Are you dealing with a stressful situation? Are you on the verge of breaking up with the love of your life? Don't know how to say yes to your gal's marriage proposal? If a stressful event gives you anxiety, take a timeout instead of doing something impulsive. Use this timeout to regroup your thoughts and decide how you want to tackle this situation. It'll help you respond more attentively to that situation.

Creating an Emotional First Aid Kit

Remember, there's no one-size-fits-all approach to emotional regulation. An exercise may work for one person but doesn't benefit others in any way. So, create a personalized emotional first aid kit, including all your favorite activities and techniques to help you be in control of your emotional rollercoaster. For instance, you can add:

- Positive affirmations to boost your self-esteem (e.g., "I can do it" statements).

- Physical activities like walking, dancing, biking, yoga, and others.

- Comfort items like childhood toys, photos, blankets, or lucky charms.

- Distraction tools like your favorite movie, book, video game, or puzzle.

- Write down the things you're thankful for, and remember to be kind to yourself.

Feel free to add more items or remove the existing ones if they don't help. Only add activities that help you heal and bring your emotions under control.

These simple exercises will make you an emotionally stabilized person. Regulating your emotions is imperative if you're looking for secure attachment. Next, you'll use all these techniques to tackle your fear of intimacy and improve your inner romantic.

Closeness and Fear - A Paradoxical Relationship

How do you feel about your relationship? Do you desire intimacy and closeness with the love of your life, yet simultaneously, you're afraid of it? Your heart is like a beautiful but delicate fortress; you want to share it with the man or woman of your dreams, but you also wonder if it's big enough for the two of you.

This conflicting desire for closeness and freedom is prevalent in folks with avoidant tendencies. In avoidant attachment, you feel (Mohammadi et al., 2016):

- Anxious about intimacy.

- Unresponsive to their partner's needs.

- Not too sensitive to their partner's feelings.

- Suffering from marital problems frequently.

Can there be a romantic relationship without the grains of love? Unfortunately, people with avoidant tendencies are looking for exactly this kind of relationship. So, let's see how a love-and-hate relationship with intimacy leads to relationship conflicts.

A Love and Hate Relationship with Intimacy: An Annoying Paradox

Imagine your partner is head over heels in love with you. They think the world of you and expect you to reciprocate similar feelings. How would they feel if you kept pulling away, pushing them out, acting all closed-off, and never being vulnerable with them?

They – quite reasonably – feel betrayed, confused, and distressed. They'll feel like you're sending them mixed messages, desiring their companionship but shutting them out.

Here's a simple exercise to see if you're sending your partner mixed signals. On a scale of 1 to 10, how do you rate your current relationship? Are you satisfied?

- You're afraid to be intimate.
- You can't recognize your or someone else's emotions.
- Your mind thinks intimacy equals vulnerability.
- You don't like making long-term commitments.
- You think you don't deserve to be loved.
- When a relationship gets serious, you get anxious.
- You don't respond well to negative emotions (we tackled this beast).

- You don't appreciate it when people try to offer emotional support (because you think they're trying to take away your independence).

- You even become violent in your relationships.

- You keep changing sexual partners (you can't stick to one due to your fear of long-term commitment and intimacy).

- You aren't very excited about sharing personal thoughts with your partner.

- You are afraid of being smothered by love, raising your fear of vulnerability.

If these symptoms hold true for you, then you may have a paradoxical relationship with your partner. We can better understand it with the help of an interesting example.

Bojack Horseman, Avoidant Attachment Manifest

It's every psychologist's favorite exercise to review fictional TV/movie characters and see what sort of behaviors they exhibit. Since we're discussing attachment styles, it would be very revealing (and also lots of fun!) to discuss another fictional character dealing with avoidant tendencies.

I have watched the show Bojack Horseman four to five times on Netflix. It's refreshing how realistically the creators portrayed mental health decline in an anthropomorphic horse. We can also see that Bojack was going through avoidant attachment.

Here are three avoidant behaviors I noticed in him:

- Just like Chandler from Friends, Bojack Horseman scampers

away from intimacy like it's the bubonic plague. He will push people away and sabotage his romantic relationships because he both needs and is afraid of intimacy. Whenever a person comes too close to meet the real Bojack, Bojack will get out of that relationship, even though he needs to be loved.

- His prize possession is his independence, his self-reliance. He will do anything to preserve his "freedom" – which is, in reality, nothing more than loneliness – to the point of hurting other people. He also struggles to emotionally support his friends, romantic partners, and other people in his life.

- He's also dismissive of what his partners want or need from him. So, he downplays the importance of intimacy. Even a discussion about emotions will set him off. The moment he feels the conservation is gravitating toward their relationship dynamics, he'll deflect.

It took Bojack a lot of whacky adventures to get the help he needed. But you've got all the help you need right here. Remember cognitive reframing? We just talked about it a while ago. It can also help you overcome your fear of intimacy and start approaching every relationship without a shiver in your bones.

A Callback to Cognitive Restructuring

Feeling disoriented about intimacy? Don't want to be an open book but also hungry for love? Cognitive restructuring can help you overcome your fear of closeness. It's all about shifting your perception of intimacy.

Does your brain make it look like a source of threat and discomfort? Shift your perspective to start seeing intimacy as a source of love and compassion. Here's how to do it:

- What negative perceptions do you have about intimacy? Identify these negative thoughts. For instance, you may think, "Intimacy will make me lose my freedom" or "Showing vulnerability will make me an easy target."

- Now, challenge these bad thoughts. Don't accept them as scripture. "Am I afraid of intimacy because of bad experiences in the past? How would I start viewing it differently?" Tell yourself that your fear of intimacy is holding you back.

- Next, replace negative thoughts with positive ones. Tell yourself that you can be intimate and still keep your identity. "Intimacy will deepen my connections and make me closer to my partner," keep repeating this mantra in your head.

- There's no need to rush it; practice intimacy in baby steps. Start by sharing a few tidbits from your "mind palace," but don't reveal your innermost thoughts at this point. Slowly, you'll learn to share more as you'll notice the life-changing benefits of being intimate, e.g., having a healthy emotional connection with your partner.

That's how you can literally change your mind about intimacy and start seeing it as a very amazing growth opportunity. Don't forget to seek professional support and try couples counseling. A therapist's office will serve as a safe space where you'll learn that it's okay to be a little vulnerable in your lover's presence and see intimacy as a blessing.

Remember the different exercises we discussed before? I deliberately left out a very important one: mindfulness. It's one of the most

important and effective tools in the arsenal of avoidant attachment recovery. Let's see how mindfulness can help you alter your attachment style.

Mindful and the Rainbow-Colored Road to Recovery

If you want to escape the maze of avoidant attachment toward the open castle of secure attachment, make mindfulness or related meditative exercises part of your daily routine. Here's how it helps you:

- It makes you grounded in the present.
- It helps to stay in touch with reality.
- It keeps you from acting impulsively.
- It decreases your emotional reactivity.

Whether you want to attain emotional awareness or enhance emotional regulation, your go-to method should always be mindfulness. Since avoidant tendencies make it hard for people to recognize their or someone else's emotions, mindfulness will help them form a deeper connection with their inner selves. After a few tailored mindfulness exercises, you won't be out of touch with your feelings and emotions.

Here's how mindfulness helps people with avoidant attachment. If you practice it, you will see the following benefits:

- You learn to live in the moment and not the past.
- You stop overthinking stuff or getting paranoid about your partner.
- As a result, you don't distance yourself emotionally from your

lover anymore.

In this section, we'll discuss how to practice mindfulness to target your avoidant and intimacy-hesitant behaviors. With enough practice, you'll be able to push away avoidant tendencies like earwax.

Mindfulness Practices to Remove Avoidant Tendencies

If you ask me to name the best tool for overcoming avoidant attachment, I'd day mindfulness without hesitation. Even research shows that mindful practices increase your resilience and make regulating your emotions easier (Yang et al., 2022).

Are you feeling overwhelmed and unable to make an important decision? Can't you feel the Earth beneath your feet? Try mindfulness and overcome emotional distress.

Here are three basic mindful practices you should follow in everyday life. Once you get mastery over these simple exercises, it'd be like having access to a magic potion that can heal your avoidant tendencies in a single mouthful:

- **Focused Breathing:** Place one hand on your belly and start breathing from the diaphragm. Focus on how your hand moves as the tummy goes up and down, like a baby sleeping. Place the other hand on your chest and ensure it doesn't move as much. The idea is that people breathe from their chests when they're anxious. So, focused breathing helps you breathe slowly and overcome your anxiety.

- **Sensory Mindfulness:** We all have five senses, right? But how often do we pay them any special attention? In sensory mindfulness, you notice what your senses are feeling. The things you see, hear, smell, taste, and touch – focus on it all. Just be like Spiderman and harness your "spidey senses." It'll help you live in the moment and always be there in the present.

- **Mindful Observation:** I'd like to call it the Rosetta stone of mindfulness. In the art of mindful observation, you simply observe what you see around you simply as a neutral observer. Be like the Watcher from the *What If...?* series. Your job is to concentrate on what's happening without judgment. It harnesses your ability to notice things without immediately rejecting or accepting them.

These beneficial practices will help change your avoidant tendencies. You will learn very slowly and gently to engage with your emotional side.

Incorporating Mindfulness in Daily Routines

Do you think these exercises are too much? Don't worry; you can simply incorporate the idea behind these different exercises into your everyday life. Check these simple tips and learn how to find time off your busy schedule to do the above three exercises:

- Take a few short breaths before getting out of the shower and starting a new day.

- Actively listen to folks when they're talking and pay attention to the conversation.

- Even when you're walking, pay attention to every step; paying attention to your bodily movements will ground you in reality.

- Eat your lunch in a distraction-free room where you can mindfully eat the food, chewing every morsel.

- Take short breaks at work and spend a few minutes alone in a room to prevent your thoughts from wandering.

- Set daily reminders to pause and check in with yourself; ask questions like, "Am I doing okay? Do I need a break from my daily routine?"

- Search for mindfulness apps online and use them to stay on track.

You may wonder how all of this helps you mend things with your partner and put your love life back on track. Let me explain the fantastic connection between mindfulness and a person's interpersonal relationships in more detail.

What Role Does Mindfulness Play in Interpersonal Interactions

If you want to improve the quality of your romantic relationships, mindfulness is the key to unlocking all the niceties necessary for a successful love life. That's not an empty promise either; several studies have shown that mindful practices can do wonders for intimate interactions (Khoury et al., 2023). Since you learn how to regulate your emotions thanks to mindfulness, you can:

- Easily accept when you're in the wrong.

- Increase your aptitude to engage in self-change.

- Pay more attention to your partner's needs and feelings.

- Never lose focus of what's important, i.e., your mutual love.

- Be mentally present in every conservation with your partner.

- Form more meaningful and connected relationships with people.

- Become a more kind and caring person, in tune with her feelings.

Combined with emotional awareness and regulation tips, these mindful practices will be your go-to tools for escaping the prison of avoidant attachment. Keep on reading as we uncover more secrets of attaining the perfect balance between your longing for freedom and your desire for intimacy.

Never let go of the strong rope of mindfulness in your life. Use it to open up a gateway to emotional excellence. It will make you more in tune with not just your but also your partner's emotions. That's how you embark on the next phase of your journey.

Key Takeaways

- Emotional attunement helps you recognize, understand, and validate your lover's feelings.

- Emotional check-ins, labeling, and body scanning are great ways to enhance your emotional awareness powers.

- Use breathing, cognitive reframing, and muscle relaxation techniques to regulate your emotions and prevent impulsive behaviors.

- Cognitive reframing is good for overcoming your fear of intimacy and embracing your desire for romantic affiliations.

- Incorporate exercises like sensory mindfulness and mindful observation into your everyday life to enjoy a healthier love life.

Sneak Peak - What's in Chapter 3?

You've learned the art of emotional awareness and beaten another monster in this quest. Another one bites the dust, I guess! So, what's next in our journey? Here's what you will learn in the next chapter:

- How to open up and communicate with your lover?

- Embracing your vulnerability as a newfound strength.

- Balancing autonomy with romantic relationships.

- Connecting with friends, family, and coworkers.

So, keep on reading and learn how to come to terms with your fear of vulnerability.

Chapter 3 - Step 3

Effective Communication and Embracing Vulnerability

> "When people talk, listen completely... You should be able to go into a room and when you come out know everything that you saw there and not only that. If that room gave you any feeling, you should know exactly what it was that gave you that feeling."
>
> Ernest Hemingway

Welcome to the third phase of our journey together. Your transformation into a more securely attached person is halfway done. You have learned to let people in and open up to them emotionally. In Chapter 3, you will find out how to turn vulnerability into your strong suit. So, let's get started with the third stage of this journey, shall we?

Priti's Story

Meet Priti; she's a shy 26 woman in an on-and-off relationship with her boyfriend, James. But she's always been avoidantly attached – the roots of her behavior go back to her childhood. Growing up in a house with nine siblings wasn't easy; Priti was always the least of her father's worries, overshadowed by more accomplished sisters.

She learned to keep to herself and mind her own business. While her avoidant behavior made her self-reliant and helped her cope with abandonment issues, it also crippled her communication skills. She sucks at expressing her emotions. That's the main reason why her relationship with James never seems to work out.

When he wants to talk, she tends to go back to her shell of minding her own business. When conversations touch on her deeper emotions or the future of the relationship, she tends to shut down. But one day, she realizes that she needs to make some changes.

Not-So-Fantastic Communication Barriers and Where to Find Them?

What does Priti do? Well, for starters, she picks up a book about avoidant tendencies and starts reading. This section is a brief account of what she learned about her avoidant tendencies and how to manage her lack of communication skills.

Priti realizes that certain communication barriers make her unable to talk about her emotions. So, check out these common communication barriers and see if they apply to you as well:

- Are you uncomfortable with expressing your emotions?
- Do you find it hard to show your emotions?
- Is it too embarrassing for you to show your emotional side?

How do these barriers play out in real life? Priti notices that she tends to:

- Avoid difficult conversations.

- Deflect hard-to-handle topics.

- Avoid dealing with other people's emotions.

- Get visibly disturbed when her partner brings up delicate topics.

Like Priti, you need to acknowledge that these barriers exist and that they make you very bad at communication. Your avoidant tendencies will only get stronger if you don't do anything to remove these communication barriers.

Effective Communication 101

Next, Priti learned the foundational principles of good communication. Spoiler alert: Merely talking doesn't make you good at communicating; you also need to listen. In the words of Hemingway, listen completely when someone is speaking.

So, here are the key pillars of effective communication for avoidant individuals:

- Clarity (the goal of communication is to be understood, so don't mince your words and be clear about what you're saying).

- Active listening is sometimes called the "highest level of listening" (Jahromi et al., 2016).

- Assertiveness, i.e., be bold and even brazen about what you're feeling; don't let anyone dismiss you easily.

- Be honest about what you want, even if it makes you uncomfortable; transparency is the root of effective communication.

Want to be better at communicating your thoughts and feelings? Priti learned these tips for better communication. They'll hopefully help you, too.

- Watch your tone; a bad tone can alter the whole message.
- Be concise; long talks tend to lose the listener's attention.
- Prepare a statement so you can talk more confidently.
- Body language and gestures are also part of communication.
- Use emotional awareness to see how well the listener is taking your message.

I hope these tips will make you an excellent communicator.

Overcome Avoidance with Effective Communication

Is there any way to overcome your avoidant tendencies with good communication? Yes, Priti learned a few very simple ways to use effective communication as a means to alter her attachment style. After all, good communication skills are a flag bearer of secure attachment, aren't they?

She tried the Gottman exercise described in Chapter 2, where you use "I" statements to have a heart-to-heart with your partner. You express your emotions without judging the other person or accusing them of anything.

Does verbal communication still make you uncomfortable? Then, write down your inner thoughts and feelings. Use journaling as a medium of self-expression.

Communication-Boosting Exercises for Avoidant Attachment

In the end, she found some awesome controlled exercises to boost her confidence, get good at communication, and express her thoughts more clearly, such as:

- Identify your emotions and what triggers them. Then, you can use "I" statements in a conversation to take ownership of your feelings. So, don't say to your partner, "You make me feel small and unimportant;" instead, say this: "When our mutual conversations are interrupted, it makes me feel unimportant."

- Again, active listening will come in handy when communicating with your partner. It helps you understand their perspective. Listen to your partner and paraphrase it in your words. Suppose your partner says they feel like you don't care about their feelings. You could respond with, "It seems like you're feeling invalidated, right? You don't feel heard."

- If you need some time off for self-reflection, communicate your boundaries to your partner calmly yet assertively. Suppose you need some "me time" to relax and recharge. You could tell your partner, "I value the time we spend in each other's company, but right now, I need to be alone. Can we please schedule some time apart?"

- It's never too late to seek feedback from your partner, family, and friends about how well you're communicating. Is your communication style good enough? So, you could say, "Please tell me how to improve my communication style?" Your loved one can give you examples of times when you could've communicated in a better way. Use this feedback to go nuts on effective communication.

Using all these strategies, Priti mended her relationship with James. Thanks to the power of effective communication, she and James are in a good place right now. Realize similar benefits for yourself! Implement the tips we've discussed and watch your life transform for the better.

In the previous chapter, you learned to overcome and embrace your fear of intimacy. In this chapter, I'll teach you to do the same with vulnerability. You'll stop thinking of it as a weakness and instead accept it as one of your many strengths.

Are you tired of cowering at the mere idea of vulnerability? The time has come to introduce a major paradigm shift; find out how to get over your fear of vulnerability and embrace it as a powerful tool to spice up your love life.

You and Your Vulnerability: A Brief Self-Assessment Exercises

The first step to making sense of your vulnerability is to identify the barriers. Ask yourself these questions:

- When you think about opening up and being vulnerable, which emotions do you experience?

- Are you afraid of vulnerability due to your bad experience with it in the past?

- Why do you think you struggle to trust others with your emotions?

- What kind of people or situations make you feel uneasy with vulnerability?

- How do you react when feeling vulnerable? Maybe you tend to withdraw, become defensive, or try another coping mechanism.

The second step is to understand the depths of your emotional patterns. Ask yourself these questions:

- Think about the times when you were feeling vulnerable. Did any specific thoughts and feelings come to your mind at that time?

- What is your current coping mechanism against vulnerability? Is it effective? Does it have harmful effects on your romantic life?

- What are the recurring themes in the way you react to vulnerability emotionally? These themes may give us a peek into your emotional state.

The third step is to develop different strategies based on your experiences. Ask yourself these questions:

- What steps can you take to be more comfortable with vulnerability?

- How do you create a supportive environment that makes you willing to open up more?

- Can you think of any specific communication skills or techniques to be better at self-expression?

- Is there someone you trust enough with whom you can practice being vulnerable? Maybe this person is none other than your partner.

- Are there any fears, worries, or negative beliefs that hinder your ability to open up and be vulnerable? How do you plan to challenge this negativity?

This simple self-assessment exercise will help you understand the deeper meaning behind opening up and being vulnerable.

Vulnerability - Turning Wounds into Resilience and Strength

The key to overcoming avoidant attachment is to get in touch with your feelings. But one thing keeps you from doing that: the fear of vulnerability. You hate being criticized and judged, don't you? It is natural. Your fear of rejection, making a spectacle of yourself in public, never lets you be open about your feelings.

In simple words, you never want to face your true emotions and feelings. This is called a fear of vulnerability that prevents you from needing others. As a result:

- You always try to be perfect.

- You close yourself off to friends.

- You keep everyone at arm's length.

- You may even get depressed (Murray et al., 2021).

Does the very idea of being open about emotions embarrass you? Do your ears get red hot when you're trying to express your sentiments (probably because you don't want the world to see the inner you)? But that's just a defense mechanism.

You're protecting yourself from the world by creating a shell of emotional distance, and vulnerability feels like UV rays trying to penetrate the Earth's ozone defenses. Some common signs include:

- Sharing information embarrasses you.

- You are always wondering, "What are they thinking about me?"

- You are afraid of being neglected, rejected, or laughed at.

- You tend to be ruminative over past events or bygone conversations.

In this section, we'll explore a few myths about vulnerability, the reasons why being an open book is important, and how to be vulnerable without overexerting yourself.

Busting Common Myths about Vulnerability

What do people often get wrong about vulnerability? By people, I mean not merely the individuals with avoidant attachment but also the general public.

- *'I can avoid vulnerability.'* Nobody can avoid it.

- *'Vulnerability means letting it all out.'* No, it means sharing your private concerns with people you trust.

- *'Vulnerability isn't needed.'* You simply can't ride the train to secure attachment without it, my dear reader.

- *'Trust comes before vulnerability.'* On the contrary, vulnerability is important in building trust.

It's time to dispel these misconceptions. Vulnerability isn't a weakness; it's a normal and quintessential human experience that needs to be embraced with open heart. It helps us:

- Build meaningful connections.

- Let people understand our flaws.

- Lend authenticity to our friendships.

- Show our romantic partners that we trust them.

We'll now explore some exercises that can help you develop your vulnerability.

How to Boost Your Vulnerability in a Healthy Way

Opening up can be scary! Let's learn how to navigate vulnerability in a way that empowers you, not exposes you. A lot of people will be ready to pounce upon exposed vulnerabilities and exploit them. Building trust is key to healthy vulnerability. Consider opening up to reliable friends, confidants, or even a therapist who can offer a safe space to share. You can share your uncertainties and concerns with them so they can help you find a way out of it.

When you don't share your vulnerabilities wisely, you may (Thomas, 2016):

- Be prone to personal attacks.

- Seem unstable.

- Be portrayed as a victim.

Let's explore how to share your vulnerabilities authentically without feeling emotionally drained. You must choose the right person(s) to be vulnerable before; ask yourself, "Does this man or woman even deserve to see the real me?" This person mustn't dismiss your feelings, try to judge you, or force a solution without suggestion.

Once you find such a kindred soul, you can start taking these steps:

- Practice vulnerability in safe spaces, i.e., in the presence of your family, friends, and lover.

- Always start small and disclose snippets from your innermost thoughts with other people.

- Establish trust through vulnerability and grow the courage to share more with the person you love.

- Slowly, you'll learn to recognize where it's safe for the hidden you to come out of the shell and share a glimpse of your authentic self.

It's equally important to understand your emotions and validate your experiences. Developing self-compassion will naturally increase your desire for closeness with others. This, in turn, will help you dismantle your defenses and become more open to vulnerability. Ultimately, self-compassion paves the way for secure attachment.

Priti is a living-and-breathing success story here. It significantly improved her sense of self-awareness and enabled her to form deeper connections with her lover. Priti also earned a greater capacity for empathy and compassion. In short, she learned to:

- Come out of the protective shell.

- Open up to her boyfriend.

- Communicate honestly.

- Rekindle her romantic life.

Remember, a successful love life requires you to be vulnerable. True love isn't afraid of sharing feelings and emotions. So, learn to be an open book in the presence of your partner, and use vulnerability as your strong suit in any relationship.

In the next section, we'll explore how to balance your need for independence with your desire for connection. You can be self-reliant and be intimate with your loved ones. Keep on reading to know the secret of autonomous connectivity.

Striking a Balance between Autonomy and Connectedness

We've come full circle to the same old discussion, i.e., the everlasting battle between your longing for connectedness and the fear of losing your identity. In avoidant attachment, it can be very challenging to move toward the seemingly distant room of connectedness by letting go of the comfy couch of autonomy.

However, just as you need to strike a balance between your work life and private affairs, it's equally important to create an equilibrium between autonomy and intimacy. Sadly, like the concept of vulnerability, autonomy also gets a bad reputation, and people have certain unfounded notions about what it entails.

So, we'll discuss the concepts of autonomy and interdependence in this section. Let's see what these ideas actually are in terms of romantic relationships.

Autonomy: Don't mistake it for emotional detachment; autonomy means your partner has to respect your boundaries. You don't lose the individual in romantic relationships, and your partner shouldn't try to suppress your identity for the sake of "love." You still have control over your life choices and can pursue hobbies and friendships outside this relationship.

Interdependence: You and your partner should be able to address their needs as individuals. You're attached to your partner, but still, you two can make your own decisions without stepping on each other's toes. In simple words, the idea of interdependence teaches you to value your emotional connection with your partner without losing the sense of self (Clarke et al., 2023).

Don't think for a second that these two concepts are mutually exclusive. Both of them are essential ingredients of healthy romantic ties. You can't function without both of these tools in your backpack.

Next, we'll explore a few reasons why both autonomy and interdependence are important. Hopefully, it'll help you understand how embracing the idea of connectivity lets you maintain your individuality and makes you successful in a relationship.

Autonomy: Never Give Up Your Identity

Do you now realize what autonomy is and what makes it different from isolation? It's not the act of shutting yourself out and acting like a closed book. Autonomy means you have to retain your identity. It means three things, in general:

- Choice

- Freedom

- Control

Keeping your identity alive after engaging in a romantic relationship is important. You don't want to forget your individuality for the sake of love, don't you? Maintaining your individuality strengthens your relationship. It shows your partner they love the complete you, not just you as part of a couple.

Studies have shown that individuals whose autonomy needs are met do better romantically. Success in one's love life depends on both partners retaining their freedom to some extent (Oz-Soysal et al., 2024). You are autonomous in a relationship if you:

- Pursue hobbies of your own.

- Take control of your own actions.

- Have freedom in decision-making to some extent.

You can see that even securely attached people have a "me time." They too often need a few moments alone. When you complete your transformation from avoidant to secure attachment, you won't lose your identity or your sense of self-reliance.

Interdependence: Shared Success is Real Success

Interdependence is the other major ingredient of a healthy, happy, romantic relationship. In this scenario, you and your partner will contribute to each other's well-being, never letting one person down so the other can rise to the occasion.

If you and your partner are interdependent, you two will:

- Listen to each other actively.

- Respect each other's boundaries.

- Make important decisions together.

- Support each other emotionally in dire times.

- Take responsibility for your own shortcomings.

- Communicate properly with each other.

- Never be afraid to be vulnerable in other's presence.

- Enjoy a heightened sense of self-esteem.

Also, interdependence isn't codependence, where you can't even function without your partner; it's an unhealthy relationship characterized by poor self-esteem and a lack of goals or desires outside the relationship. It kind of reminds me of Jerry and Beth from the sci-fi show Rick and Morty, who:

- Try to control each other.

- Can't communicate properly.

- Wallow in self-pity and blame each other.

- Engage in people-pleasing behaviors.

- Can't connect with each other emotionally.

This relationship is the complete opposite of autonomy. Secure attachment thrives on a healthy balance between connection and independence. While complete enmeshment can be stifling, so can a lack of closeness. Aim to create a partnership where you both feel supported and can still pursue your own interests.

Secure attachment in a relationship flourishes when there's a beautiful balance between independence and togetherness. You can be both a strong individual and a supportive partner. There's no need to sacrifice your identity for love or your connection for personal growth. Keep both aspects of your personality equally balanced.

Intimacy and Connectedness - Beyond Romantic Affiliations

I bet you thought these tips and tricks only apply to romantic flings, didn't you? Let me tell you, dear reader, that the principles of open communication are universal. The importance of open communication goes beyond romantic partners. It's a cornerstone for building strong relationships with friends, family, and colleagues, too. That's because these principles can enhance any relationship, romantic or simply amicable. Why is that?

That's because when you show vulnerability, you're essentially communicating with all the people around you. Here's how it happens:

- You talk about how you feel the way you do.
- You discuss the reasons why you feel the way you do.
- You let others understand where you're coming from.
- You openly express your thoughts and perspectives.
- They develop empathy for you.

You can see how vulnerability makes communication powerful, driving trust and empathy in every relationship. I can practically sense your suspicion. How does it help to be vulnerable – open about your emotional scars and psychological wounds – in front of the people you work with? Well, I have the perfect case study for you.

Rosa Diaz: The Importance of Vulnerability at Work

I'm not ashamed to say that Brooklyn Nine-Nine (B99) has always been a guilty pleasure of mine. I connected with these cops and enjoyed how their adventures protected the streets of Brooklyn from dirty criminals.

While my friends were obsessed with the characters of Jake Peralta and Capt Ray Hold – who is everyone's favorite, not gonna lie – I was in awe of Rosa Diaz, one of the best depictions of avoidant attachment on modern television.

- While she's hesitant to open up about her love life, she learns to talk about it little by little, starting with telling her pals merely the name of her partner.

- She grows from a person who doesn't even share her home address with people to giving her coworkers a glimpse of her private life.

- She opens up about her bisexuality and the problems she's faced with her family because of it.

- She slowly starts to share the details of her romantic life with her coworkers.

- When her boyfriend gets kidnapped, she opens up about how she's afraid of losing him.

Hopefully, Rosa's example has helped to see how applying the principles of vulnerability in communication can enhance any relationship.

Vulnerability in Communication with Friends and Work Buddies

When was the last time your friends had a heart-to-heart? Don't be afraid to discuss any deep-seated fears and insomnia-inducing concerns with your friends. It's completely fine to admit fears or insecurities and talk about how afraid you are of something. Here's a straightforward exercise to check if you're communicating well with your pals:

- Do you usually express concerns with your friends?

- Do you often share personal achievements with them?

- Do you talk to them about your personal life?

- Do you take them in confidence when making important decisions?

Showing vulnerability will deepen your friendships. It will also allow your friends to be vulnerable and open up to you about their feelings, leading to mutual emotional support and growth. Maybe one of your friends is growing through tough times. When they will see you opening up about your concerns, it'll give them the courage to seek help.

Even in professional settings, showing vulnerability is important for your productivity. So, you should be open about how much of a workload suits you. Don't be afraid to say, "I don't know how to do this," and seek someone's help. It'll lead to these fantastic benefits:

- Increasing your self-awareness.

- Better decision-making capabilities.

- Demonstrating the strength of your character.

- Showing how honest and frank you are.

- Letting you share the stress of your job with the manager.

They say, "Sharing is caring," and this saying rings true in the context of workplace relationships as well.

Again, I should remind you to avoid oversharing. There's a difference between healthy vulnerability and oversharing. Sharing deeply intimate things and overtly personal information can be problematic. It might make others uncomfortable. So, we need to talk about setting boundaries. Also, it's equally important to clarify to your friends that you will decide when to open up to them. Don't let someone force you to be vulnerable; be vulnerable when you feel the time is right.

Setting Boundaries When Communicating

While Rosa Diaz is an excellent example of how to open up about your feelings, Jake Peralta's best friend Boyle is a fine example of how not to show vulnerability. This is what he does wrong:

- Overstepping boundaries by sharing overly personal information.

- Excessively talking about his passions and interests.

- Forcing his coworkers to be equally as vulnerable as he is.

- Unabashedly asking people about their private lives.

Setting visible and clear boundaries is essential when you're trying to communicate your feelings. That's especially true in workplace communication. For instance, strangers shouldn't meddle in your private affairs, and casual friends shouldn't ideally ask deep and personal questions. Here is how you can communicate your boundaries at work:

- "I don't have the energy to help you out with [--------] at this moment."

- "I don't have the emotional capacity to listen to [--------] right now."

- "It makes me uncomfortable when you do [--------], so I have to leave."

- "[---------] is not a topic I want to discuss with you right now."

- "I am not okay with you sharing my story on social media."

In short, you must not be afraid to let people see your soft side. It makes you easier to talk to and prevents you from burning out under the burden of unspoken emotions. But it's equally important to choose what to reveal and who to share your feelings with. Also, respect other people's emotional margins if you expect them to respect yours.

Now, you know that the concept of vulnerability applies to friendships, too. It isn't restricted to romantic relationships. Next, we'll discuss how people with avoidant attachments can reach out to people, make new friends, and be the ones to initiate friendships. Stay tuned and expand your social circle.

Expand Your Social Circle - The Bridge to Secure Attachment

We've arrived at the last section of Chapter 3: The fine art of communicating effectively with people. You may wonder how to expand your social circle and make new friends. How do you initiate conversations? How do you extend the first hand of friendship? How do you make new and long-lasting connections without overwhelming yourself?

You may get overwhelmed by the idea of making new friends. As a person with avoidant tendencies, you may have shown these features (Thompson et al., 2023):

- Withdrawing from friendships to avoid intimacy.
- Not taking any initiative in forming friendships.
- Breaking friendships out of the fear of vulnerability.
- Avoiding friendships due to abandonment issues.

Don't worry; I'll explain how to form new friendships and always be the first to initiate a new amicable relationship. You can now expand your social circle and start the move toward secure attachment at a faster pace.

Good Communication Demands Baby Steps

There's no need to go fast and all in! Take baby steps. That's how you can get in the zone and prevent burnout. I'm not asking you to do something you're uncomfortable with right away. Maybe you're more comfortable creating a Facebook account and making new friends online.

It would help if you always started small. Let's explore some easy first steps towards building friendships, all at your own pace! There's no need to rush out of your comfort zone:

- Feeling shy? Start with group activities where there's no pressure on you to be the one to start the conversation. They offer a relaxed environment where you can connect with others through shared interests, and you're not pressured to have one-on-one conversations right away. This allows you to ease into meeting new people at your own pace.

- Don't invest too much energy in forming new friendships right away. Always set clear-cut personal boundaries. Take your time to find people who share your values and make you feel good.

- Then, focus on nurturing these new friendships. It's always better to have a few nice friends than lots of random acquaintances. Strengthen these bonds first and then move on to expanding your circle of friends further.

Remember, it's not about increasing your number of friends in the real world. We aren't talking about LinkedIn or X (formerly Twitter) here, where your number of followers matters. In real-world settings, true friendships involve a deep understanding, trust, and mutual support. Even if you manage to find one true friend out there among 8 billion souls, you've done well.

Making new friends is key to altering your attachment style. However, you can't make new pals without communicating the right way. So, let's review some fantastic tips to be excellent at communicating with strangers.

How to Communicate Well? A Few Useful Techniques

Are you still overwhelmed by closeness? Is the idea of intimacy something you're working through? Don't fret; There are two strategies to help you communicate well despite your fear of connectedness:

1. **Active Listening:** It simply means paying attention to what the other person is saying. Active listening is an integral part of effective communication. It helps build empathy and creates a bond of understanding between two people without the need to be overtly

vulnerable. If you don't want to disclose too much information, try active listening to make new connections without overwhelming yourself.

2. **Nonverbal Communication:** What happens when your body language shows you aren't interested in a conversation? Focus on nonverbal cues like gestures and facial expressions. Open body language is a welcoming sign and shows how friendly you are. Maintain eye contact when listening to someone and nod to show you're engaged.

Try these tips to excel as a communicator. But don't forget to set boundaries; after all, a new friend must show they can value your privacy and independence.

Healthy Boundaries for Independence and Connectedness

Remember, secure attachment isn't about losing your independence and being 100% vulnerable. It's about striking a balance between the two extremes of ultimate freedom and warts-and-all-nothing-off-the-books frankness. You must set healthy boundaries to ensure people respect your need for privacy.

Here's what you should remember about boundaries:

- Setting boundaries is your right, and there's no need to apologize for it! You choose who you open up to and how much.

- Communicate your boundaries to others assertively. Be very clear that you don't want to talk about a certain topic or discuss private affairs with a casual friend.

- Use polite, clear, and assertive words when conveying the need for the "me time." Say, "I value your company, but right now I need some space," "It's always good to talk to you, but I want to be alone right now," or "Please give me time to myself to recharge, and we'll talk later."

It goes without saying – it's equally important to respect someone else's boundaries. Even your partner may need space and ask for some "me time." Maybe they miss their friends and hang out with them. Or, there are some topics they can only discuss freely with their parents and siblings. In a secure, avoidant-free relationship, you will respect your loved one's privacy by:

- Honoring their needs for freedom and "me time."

- Not feeling rejected by their yearning to be alone for a while.

- Not feeling distant when they try to connect to you later.

Hopefully, you now understand that good communication is a matter of give and take. You have to give up some of your freedom by showing a few glimpses of vulnerability; as a reward, you receive people's trust and get to see them opening up to you.

Empowered with these simple tips and strategies, you are now ready to go on this exciting quest and use communication tools to build healthy connections and move beyond avoidant attachment. Just remember to spread your wings thin and start small.

Key Takeaways

- Recognize common communication barriers, e.g., deflecting specific topics.

- Learn the pillars of good communication: clarity, honesty, assertiveness, and active listening.

- Realize that you can't live without showing vulnerability; it's key to alter your attachment style.

- Practice vulnerability in baby steps; reach out to trusted friends, divulge bits of info, and establish trust.

- Embrace autonomy and interdependence, the two pillars of secure attachment.

- Learn that the need for intimacy and connectedness goes far beyond romantic ties; you should also work on expanding your social circle.

- Openness is key, but it's important to find a balance.

What's Next in Chapter 4?

We're more than halfway done, right? That's a relief. Well, you're now closer to altering your attachment style – much closer than ever before. We can move on to the 4th stage in our journey. Here's what awaits you in the next chapter:

- Intimacy challenges you might face due to avoidant issues.

- How do you express your feelings to your partner?

- A step-by-step guide to building intimate connections.

- Showing physical affection made easy.

Want to sweep your lover off their feet? We've got some winning communication strategies to help you build a deeper connection!

Chapter 4 - Step 4
Intimacy and Affection

> "Real intimacy is only possible to the degree that we can be honest about what we are doing and feeling."
>
> Joyce Brothers

Finally, we're drawing closer to your transformation into a securely attached person. This is the fourth stage of our journey together. In this chapter, you will learn the subtle art of intimacy and find the proper way to express your love for your partner.

Individuals with avoidant attachment often struggle with showing intimacy. They have a hard time expressing affection or telling their loved ones how much they care. Don't you get annoyed when your avoidant tendencies stop you from expressing intimacy like all other couples?

Miriam feels torn between her desire for intimacy and freedom. Growing up as the only child of a bedridden mother and deadbeat father, she was raised by an awesome stepdad who was always there for her – except when he was engulfed in his job, working as a traveling salesman. She learned to live alone, constantly fighting off heart-crunching concerns about her ailing mother.

She was so afraid to lose her mom that she distanced herself from her emotions. But assuming a stoic attitude toward life's barrage of miseries didn't do her much good either. She lost the ability to articulate her emotions openly; intimacy became a concept lost to poor little Miriam.

Now, she's a grown woman, working for a telemarketing agency. She is a good worker and has many friends. But while she's doing great on many frontiers of life, her love life is filled with hiccups and setbacks. She always imagined an ideal wedding as a kid – she would be dressed in white, walking down the aisle with her stepdad, and her partner's face would drop at the sight of her angelic face.

Miriam is in her late 30s and has no idea what went wrong. "What did I do? Where did I go wrong?" She practically had no idea about her avoidant tendencies until she met a counselor and learned what it means to be avoidantly attached.

We'll see what she learned and how she started her journey toward secure attachment. First, let's take a brief look at intimacy as a concept.

Intimacy: The Concept and its Multifaceted Dimensions

You may understand "intimacy" as a fleeting passion that leads to reproduction. But in reality, it's far more complex than the major driving force behind a healthy sex life. You express intimacy when you feel close to someone, as if there's a special bond between you and that other person.

Psychologists believe intimacy in terms of romantic relationships means five ideas (van Lankveld et al., 2018):

   1. Love

2. Warmth

3. Sexual intimacy

4. Tenderness

5. Connectedness

But don't think that intimacy is something physical; it's about connecting with your lover and being vulnerable in their presence. It's also about sharing not just thoughts or feelings but entire experiences.

- **Physical:** You hug and kiss your partner, cuddle with them, and find comfort in their presence. When your partner touches you, you feel safe and find pleasure in this physical connection.

- **Emotional:** You and your partner can share their innermost thoughts when they are alone. You enjoy a bond of trust and empathy with them. You feel safe to be vulnerable in front of your lover.

- **Intellectual:** You can talk with your partner about literally anything. It's all about stimulating each other's minds and sharing ideas without mocking each other.

- **Experimental:** You share experiences with your partner. You guys travel and explore new hobbies together. You like spending quality time with each other and creating shared new memories.

Sadly, Miriam and many other women like her struggle to be intimate on an emotional level. She feels uncomfortable with emotional closeness and always prioritizes freedom over connection. That's because her instincts tell her to create distance from those who love her. Subconsciously, she's afraid she might lose her autonomy in pursuit of love.

Consider these two scenarios:

- Your significant other wants you two to spend more time together. But your fear of engulfment is in the way; you don't want to lose yourself in the relationship, so you grow anxious and withdraw.

- If you have experienced betrayal in a previous relationship, it might be difficult for you to trust others. Emotional scars run deep and force you to push your lover away. While you think your mistrust of people is protecting you, actually, it's just ruining your chances at a healthy love life.

But there's no need to lose hope. Do what Miriam did and get your romantic liaisons back on track. Try out these simple exercises to overcome all barriers to intimacy:

- Take some time to reflect on your fears and apprehensions. Ask yourself, "Which past experiences influence my current behavior?" Probably something from your childhood? Abandonment issues? Abusive exes? Once you find the root causes of these barriers to intimacy, addressing them won't be an issue.

- Once again, you'll learn how to communicate your boundaries to your partner calmly and respectfully. Ask them to give you some space and let you open up to them on your own terms.

- Do you have a nurturing and supportive environment where you can be vulnerable and share your innermost thoughts? Maybe a friend, family member, or therapist who can provide empathy and understanding?

It all starts with building trust in small steps. Healing needs to come naturally to you. There's no need to rip the Band-Aid off or try to rush the process. Here's what you have to do:

- Start by sharing minor, harmless details about your life. A funny story from work or personal anecdotes. A non-threatening piece of information will do. It makes you comfortable to share more intimate stuff with your partner later on.

- Play games like Two Truths and A Lie, in which you and your partner will tell two truths and one lie about each other. The other person has to guess which one's the lie. It's a lighthearted way to build trust by sharing information.

- Give it time, and you'll slowly regain your ability to trust others.

Next, I'll share a step-by-step process for mending and building romantic ties. You will learn how to get back on your feet and take control of your love life.

A Step-by-Step Process to Build Intimate Relationships

Let's start a new journey of healing. How do you build intimacy and grow closer to your loved ones? For that, we need to hear your thoughts and understand what you mean by intimacy. Ask yourself these questions first:

- What are your relationship goals? What do you wish to achieve from this bond? Where do you see this relationship going?

- How do you define intimacy? What is your interpretation of "being intimate?"

This four-step exercise will empower you to overcome barriers to intimacy. Keep these two simple questions in mind, and you'll be well on your way to stronger connections.

Step 1: Sharing is Caring

The best way to deepen the connection with your romantic partner is to share personal stuff. It's like entrusting them with a part of your personality, deep secrets you don't feel comfortable sharing with anyone else. It shows how much you trust them and value them.

- Start with easy conversations! Share your passion for a hobby or a funny work anecdote. This creates a relaxed atmosphere for deeper conversations later.

- Once you feel comfortable sharing small stuff, practice sharing your innermost thoughts and feelings with your partner.

- After that, you can try telling them about the things that disturb you. Your fears, vulnerabilities, insecurities, bad memories, etc.

- Encourage your partner to share similar stuff about them. It'll deepen the bond that you share with each other.

Whether you want to get closer to your lover, friends, or family members, sharing these intimate details about yourself will do the trick.

Step 2: Active Listening

This topic was covered before. You need to pay attention when the other person is talking to show them how much they matter to you. In simple words, it's about validating your loved one's feelings and experiences. Here's how Miriam did it and made her partner feel heard:

- Her partner talks about how a customer accused her of giving her the wrong pair of shoes at the shoe store.

- She makes eye contact to show that she's listening.

- To show that she's engaged in the conversation, Miriam nods occasionally; her partner then knows they aren't just talking to a wall.

- She asks appropriate questions and makes harmless comments like, "It seems like you were in a difficult situation." or "You really handled it poorly, I think."

- She asks for clarification and summarizes some parts of the story to show that you're invested in the story. She says, "In the end, the manager realized you were right, and the customer was just being an idiot."

- She shows empathy and offers emotional support by saying, "It must have been a tough day for you."

Step 3: Shared Activities

Even shared experiences can help you and your partner rediscover that spark and grow closer to each other. In Miriam's case, she realizes that her passion for anime cosplaying is something she shares with her partner, who is an otaku like her.

This discovery brought them closer to each other and became a great excuse for them to spend time together and get to know each other. Studies show that couples who spend a lot of time talking to each other and engage in shared activities (Hogan et al., 2021):

- Grow closer to each other.
- Are more satisfied with the relationship.
- Perceive their relationship in a more positive light.

So, find excuses to talk to your partner and be with them whenever possible.

Step 4: Rising from Challenges

Have you fought with your partner and don't know how to deal with it? Relax, every couple fights. A healthy relationship isn't about how often you fight but how you resolve these conflicts.

Take Miriam as an example again. Her partner once made plans with friends without asking for Miriam's input. Even though Miriam was hurt, she decided to constructively discuss the problem with her partner. Here's how the conversation went.

Miriam: "I felt excluded and neglected by your actions."

Partner: "I didn't mean to ignore you, I just wanted to hang out with friends."

Miriam: "I understand. Let's hang out sometimes, only us."

Partner: "Nothing will make me happier."

See? This is how you can resolve any conflict with your partner. Hey, disagreements happen! But instead of letting anger take the wheel, try talking things out calmly. Finding common ground is way better than yelling at each other.

If you want to create deeper relationships with your loved ones, especially your spouse or partner, keep applying these simple strategies to your life. It will make your love life more meaningful, taking you deeper into the warm oceans of intimacy. The key to a happy sex life is to understand the fundamentals of intimacy by using the strategies enshrined in this section.

Don't forget that building intimacy is an ongoing process and takes time. It doesn't just require your efforts; your partner should also be involved in it. That's why, in the next section, we'll discuss how to make your lover part of the healing process.

Involving Your Partner - The Foundation of Intimacy

In the everlasting words of Joyce Brothers, intimacy is about honesty; we need to be honest about our feelings and actions. But it isn't enough if only one person is trying to be honest and vulnerable. A relationship is like a bicycle; both wheels need to work harmoniously for the bicycle to progress on the road.

Similarly, your partner needs to take part in this intimacy-building exercise too. Only then can you alter your attachment style and move from avoidant to secure.

Here's what your partner does for you:

- They support you emotionally during the journey.
- They are the receiver of your innermost thoughts.
- They help you hone your communication skills.
- They respect your boundaries, making you feel safe.
- They give you regular feedback on your progress.

But you may ask, "Isn't this journey supposed to be deeply personal?" That's true. However, it is crucial to have a supportive partner by your side to make this transition easier. No journey, no matter how personal, is incomplete without your significant other's intimate contributions and feedback. They can support your personal growth and speed up the healing process.

Joint Reflection Sessions

So, how do you make your partner part of this journey? One exercise is called the "joint reflection session," in which you and your partner reflect on each other's feelings. You can do it like this:

- Share your feelings with your partner.

- Tell them about your negative/positive experiences.

- Listen to them when they share their feelings/experiences.

- Discuss these shared pieces of information.

This and many other simple exercises have been explored in detail in the books written on avoidant attachment. Why don't you share some academic resources with your loved one? Help them learn more about your attachment style.

Tips for Your Partner

Dealing with an avoidant partner can be exhausting, but your loved one needs a strong, supportive environment, a place where they can be vulnerable and express their needs.

Here's how you can do that:

- Listen to your avoidant partner when they have something to say.

- Validate their feelings and experience.

- Check-in with them about their well-being.

- Don't force them to be vulnerable without their consent.

For instance – and this example might seem a little too personal – surveys have shown that people with avoidant attachment avoid sexual intercourse with their partner if they feel sex makes them vulnerable and is emotionally overwhelming (van Lankveld et al., 2021).

Tackle Relationship Challenges Head-on

Here's what you need to hear about relationship building. Focus on these simple strategies to tackle any challenge that thwarts the integrity of your budding romantic ties:

- Find a safe space where you and your lover can be vulnerable without judgment.

- Share any concerns you two have with each other openly and honestly.

- Whenever a challenge arises, brainstorm possible solutions with your partner.

- Always be willing to compromise and adjust your behavior per your partner's request.

- Don't hesitate to refer to a therapist or relationship counselor when things get out of control.

You're now ready to move toward the final phase of this journey.

With your lover's hand in yours, you can walk the road of attachment, making way from avoidant to secure in record time. Just learn to embrace vulnerability, share your fears and desires with your partner, and open up to the warmth of touch.

The Warmth of Touch: How to Show Physical Affection?

We've broken down emotional barriers. Now, it's time to get physical and learn to show affection through the warmth of touch. It's a powerful way to build secure attachments. A person suffering from avoidant attachment is hesitant to physical touch; they prefer if others don't touch them or get too close. "Personal space" is a concept that is very dear to them.

So, do you tend to recoil when your partner touches you? Do unexpected touches make you uncomfortable? It's common for introverted individuals as well to view the idea of physical affection suspiciously.

However, it would help if you opened up to the warmth of touch. It is possible only if you understand how physical affection comes in various shapes, sizes, and forms. It can be:

- A pat on the back.

- A simple handshake.

- A warm hug.

- Cuddling gently.

- Kissing someone on the cheek.

- A passionate kiss.

- Fondling and pre-sex activities.

From a gentle touch to a warm embrace – there are different forms of physical affection. So, you can choose which "physical level you're okay with" right now. Maybe you will find it okay if someone shakes your hand. Or, you're OK with a simple hug. Probably, getting a quick kiss on the cheek from family members will feel "not that bad." Slowly and with time, you can teach yourself to grow more accustomed to higher levels of affection.

Physical affection is good for your well-being, too. It releases the hormone oxytocin. It is associated with a feeling of glee, happiness, and a stress-free attitude. Data shows that physical affection lowers the stress-causing chemical cortisol and boosts the production of oxytocin in your body (Schneider et al., 2023). Here is how this chemical will benefit your journey toward secure attachment:

- Your brain gets used to physical affection when it associates it with feelings of glee and happiness.

- You begin to trust your partner, and the bond between you two grows strong.

- It strengthens your sense of connection with your loved ones.

That's why you'll see that folks with secure attachments are okay with not just receiving but also expressing physical affection. Here's a fascinating study I was reading the other day. It surveyed 13 men and 27 women from different backgrounds and observed their attachment behaviors. It turns out that the warmth of touch makes a person feel a lot less lonely.

In other words, married couples suffering from loneliness and feeling like their relationship is going nowhere are – pardon me for using Internet slang – basically touch-starved. So, embracing the warmth of touch is the fastest way to reduce loneliness and speed your journey toward secure attachment (Tejada et al., 2020).

It kind of reminds me of a certain Internet phenomenon in which youngsters claim to be "kiss-less, hug-less" individuals, complaining about loneliness and mourning their highly avoidant behaviors. It seems that there really is a connection between the warmth of touch and loneliness.

That is because a "touch" isn't merely an act of making contact with another person's body with yours; it's a deeply personal act that conveys a deeper meaning. Physical affection hides the following secrets within it:

- It tells the other person, "I'm right here".

- It shows an unspoken bond of love.

- It conveys emotional support.

I would even say that receiving physical affection from your partner is a sign that there is still hope; you two can still make it work. Similarly, expressing physical affection will show you that a person with avoidant tendencies has the potential for growth. You have the room and the capacity to make everything better and work on yourself. That's how the act of touch, the warmness of physical contact, gives an unspoken yet deeply felt message to your partner.

It is a silent way of saying how much you love your partner.

But what should you do if you are touch-avoidant? How do you grow more accepting of physical contact with your loved one?

It's challenging to change your habits overnight and become desensitized to touching in a snap. You must gradually overcome your abhorrence for physical contact with your loved ones. For instance, try these exercises:

- **Hand-Holding Exercises:** Imagine you're walking side by side with your lover or friend. It's a safe environment, such as a park where you like to go to clear your mind. While you two are walking, reach out and hold the other person's hand. It may feel weird for a moment, but after a few minutes, you will enjoy touching the person you love/care about.

- **Shoulder-Rubbing Exercises:** Stand next to your lover. Ask them if you want to give them a brief massage. If they consent to the idea, you can rub their back (or have them rub yours). Relax your muscles, do deep-breathing exercises, and enjoy the experience. Slowly make this shoulder-rubbing session last longer, and you'll soon grow accustomed to it.

- **Progressive Touching:** In this exercise, you can let your partner touch you on the less sensitive body parts, such as your back and forearm. Once you stop being weird about it, you can ask them to touch you on sensitive body parts, such as the forehead, hands, neck, and belly. It'll help you overcome any anxiety or hesitancy associated with the warmth of touch.

- **Self-Touching:** Try massaging your own hands and shoulders. You can comfortably do this exercise using only your body. Slowly, you'll grow desensitized to the idea of touching and familiar with the physical sensation of being touched.

There are just a few points to remember here:

- Always ask for your partner's consent.

- Communicate your fears of physical affection to them.

- Ensure your partner is also comfortable with these exercises.

- Always start slowly.

What you can now do is create touch rituals to ensure physical affection doesn't become something you and your partner do out of the ordinary. Make it part of daily life. Try to make these simple routines the new normal in your daily habits:

- Hug your partner when greeting them.

- Kiss them before going to bed every night.

- Sit close to each other when watching a movie.

These simple strategies will make you more open to the idea of touching as a means to show your love and affection. But don't just do "touching" like a mindless activity. It needs to be meaningful; it needs to be full of emotion. So, incorporate mindfulness into the art of touching. Grab your partner's hand in your hand. What do you feel? What are your emotions?

What goes on in your head when you're being physically intimate with the love of your life? Focus on this sensation, this warmth oozing from something deep within your heart. Set your mind on this emotion to enjoy this experience. If you still do not feel at ease with physical affection, here's what you can do:

- Set boundaries with your partner by saying, "I am okay with holding hands, but hugging seems just too much right now."

- Ensure your partner knows that you're not refusing physical touch out of loathing but due to sheer aversion to the act of touching.

- Respect your boundaries, and don't pressure yourself into making physical contact.

These simple tips will make you a more touch-friendly person, opening you to a whole new world of affection and emotional connection. The warmth of touch will also speed up your transformation from avoidant to secure attachment style. And this concludes the fourth phase of our journey together.

In this section, you learned how to slowly increase your disposition toward physical closeness. The key is to ensure you're comfortable with it and only let trusted people into your "personal space." It will melt the icy remnants of your emotional state, making you more open to emotional connections.

Key Takeaways

- Intimacy has multiple dimensions, such as physical, emotional, sexual, and others.

- Share words and activities with your lover, listen to them actively, and stay strong in the face of challenges.

- Ensure your partner becomes a part of this journey as you're strong together.

- Learn to tackle relationship challenges to grow more intimate and never block the communication process.

- Embrace the warmth of touch via exercises like hand-holding, shoulder-rubbing, and self-massaging.

What's Next in Chapter 5?

We've successfully finished four out of five steps of this journey. Your transformation is nearly complete. In the final phase of this adventure, here's what you will learn:

- Celebrate the change, appreciate your efforts, and recognize the new you.

- Remember the tips you learned and make them part of this ongoing journey.

- Create a robust support system to avoid relapse (i.e., you going back to your avoidant style).

- Develop a foolproof follow-up plan and take extra good care of yourself.

So, let's see each other in Chapter 5 and finally say Sayonara to your avoidant attitude.

Chapter 5 - Step 5

Sustainable Growth and Personal Development

> "It's a funny thing about life; once you begin to take note of the things you are grateful for, you begin to lose sight of the things that you lack."
>
> Germany Kent

Welcome to the fifth stage of this quest, the stage where we complete your transformation into a secure person. Let's start by celebrating your success and hard work. Recognize the progress you've made in the past few days, going from Step 1 of the journey to Step 5. It wasn't easy reaching the finish line; I get it.

It takes a strong person with an iron will to alter their attachment style like you did! Celebrating small victories will encourage you to achieve even bigger goals (Reid, 2023).

This is the point: Don't belittle your achievements, no matter how small they seem. Even minor personality changes require a lot of hard work. Imagine sending your kid to their first day at school. You can boost their self-esteem and encourage them to excel in their academics by celebrating their first week at school, first month, sixth month, and first year.

You may think these victories are small. But, in retrospect, you'll realize these small victories lay the foundations of bigger changes. That's because:

- Your brain is wired to work with a reward-based mechanism; celebrating your small achievements is a great way to boost your sense of self-reliance.

- Tracking minor achievements will motivate you to achieve more and motivated to stay on track for the remainder of your journey.

- Celebrating smaller goals will encourage you to achieve bigger goals because your brain will find pleasure in goal achievement.

- Recognizing and consolidating change is a fantastic way to rediscover your sense of self-confidence and start believing in yourself.

After all, I always ask my clients to embrace SMART goal-setting as the go-to method to bring out major changes in their personalities. I hope you've heard of this term before. It is an acronym that stands for:

- **S**pecific

- **M**easurable

- **A**chievable

- **R**ealistic

- **T**ime-bound

Surveys show that setting SMART goals will lead to long-lasting behavioral changes and help a person alter their bad habits easily (Bailey, 2017). That's because SMART goal-setting leverages your brain's reward-dependence nature to boost your self-motivation. In other words, you will focus on bringing small changes in your personality.

Once you overcome minor manifestations of avoidant attachment, you can move on to overcoming major symptoms of avoidance. For this reason, you should celebrate your victories, no matter how small. Also, celebrate your success after achieving major milestones, such as:

- When you acknowledge that your part trauma is responsible for your avoidant attitude (Step 1).

- When you learn to regulate your emotions and balance your fear of intimacy with the desire for emotional connection (Step 2).

- When you learn to be vulnerable in a safe space and rely on others for emotional support while maintaining some degree of freedom (Step 3).

- When you overcome the barriers to physical affection and learn to embrace the warmth of touch (Step 4).

If you are still wondering why small victories matter, here's a breakdown of their major benefits:

- They make a seemingly difficult task easily manageable.

- They improve your momentum and speed up the journey.

- They make it less likely for you to resort to your bad ways.

- They create a positive feedback loop that promotes continued progress.

- They help you jump to the next stage of the journey with minimal distractions.

Now, I'm sure you are asking yourself one other question: How do you celebrate your wins? Well, I don't want to be the one to tell you how to celebrate your success. Do it the way you please. Do you want to spend some "me time" celebrating your victory? Want to have dinner alone? Looking forward to that hot shower? Thinking about taking a stroll in the park?

It's all up to you; celebrate your small victories the way you seem appropriate. But here are some general ways people in recovery, i.e., people close to the transformation from avoidant to secure attachment, tend to celebrate their achievements:

- **Say it out loud:** Talk about your winnings, tell someone, or simply tell yourself how much you've achieved.

- **Write it down:** Pick up your journal and write about it; tell dear diary how far you've come in your journey.

- **Share it online:** If it feels comfortable enough, share your success story online. Maybe it'll inspire other people with avoidant tendencies to focus on change.

- **Think about it:** Even quiet contemplation will do wonders as you reflect on how much better your life is when you don't avoid physical intimacy and are available to your partner emotionally.

These simple tips will help you turn secure tendencies into long-lasting habits. In simple words, it's all about replacing avoidant tendencies with secure ones. You should find the strategies that help you the most and facilitate the process of replacing your bad habits with good ones. This is what you should do at the final stage of this journey:

- Go through all the exercises in this book.

- Rate every exercise for helpfulness on a scale of 1 to 10 (1 indicates the exercise was not helpful at all.

- See which exercises are rated 5+ on this scale; stick to these exercises in the future.

- Make these exercises part of your daily routine, and soon, you'll notice that you do not experience avoidant tendencies at all.

Create a list of strategies that have worked for you during this journey and stick to them. One exercise may work for you but not for others. So, focus on what is helpful; prioritize that exercise and stick to it faithfully. Consistency, hard work, and gratitude – these are the three ingredients to complete your transformation into a securely attached person.

It's important to be grateful for what you've achieved. Only with a grateful mind can you hop on to the next stage of this quest, maintaining your secure attachment style. Let's see how to maintain your security and never go back to your avoidant tendencies.

Quest Forever - How to Maintain the Newfound Security?

Security isn't something you can simply achieve and keep somewhere. It's a state of mind, a continuous process that needs to be nurtured from time to time. It's a journey that never stops. You must keep building upon these secure behaviors and developing the thought patterns wired in the previous steps.

Stop thinking of secure attachment as a final destination of some sort. It's an ongoing, dynamic journey. All the steps discussed before were meant to put you on this road. You were supposed to be able to walk the path of security. With your hard work and utmost dedication, we're finally there!

You've overcome the barriers that kept you from making emotional connections and expressing yourself appropriately. In the world of attachment styles, however, progress isn't something you achieve; it's something you experience.

Your goal throughout the first four chapters was to escape the hurricanes of avoidance and enter the calm oceans of security. In the final chapter, you'll learn how to maintain your newfound security. Watch out for relapse, and don't let your avoidant tendencies make an appearance. Ask yourself these crucial questions from time to time:

- Am I detaching myself emotionally from my partner again?
- Am I uncomfortable with physical intimacy again?
- Am I failing at communicating my needs to my partner?
- Am I deliberately avoiding new friendships at work?
- Am I surrendering before my old wounds once more?

A relapse will simply undo all the progress we made in the past few chapters. So, you always need to be on guard for changes in your behavior patterns. Whenever you notice yourself going back to your old ways, you may try the following to avoid a relapse:

- Monitor your thoughts and feelings.
- Check-in with your attachment patterns.
- Watch out for major or minor changes in your behavior.

- Ask your support system to inform you if they see your behavior changing.

Whenever you find yourself relapsing, go back to the relevant chapter tackling the issue you are dealing with. For instance, let's say you start experiencing emotional regulation issues again. In this case, you'll review the relevant sections from Chapter 2.

Similarly, if you notice a change in your sensitivity to touch, such as a growing discomfort with warmth, refer back to the discussion in Chapter 4 for strategies to manage this.

However, there are some general tips to help you stay on track and avoid relapse:

- Pick up a notebook and start journaling. It will help you reflect on your thoughts, actions, and behaviors – giving you a fantastic self-reflection opportunity. It does seem a little repetitive to talk about the benefits of journaling again, but I will say this: Journaling is a great way to learn new things about how your mind works and get the hang of your complex thought patterns.

- Meditation is yet another great way to peek into the hidden corridors, labyrinths, and basements of your mind. Besides reducing anxiety, meditation can help you regulate your behavior and unlock the keys to maintaining your security forever (Krishnakumar et al., 2015). You can practice yoga to calm your mind, using this momentary calmness to understand the inner workings of your brain.

Use these simple strategies – most of which have been explored before in this guide – to assess key areas of success. Find out what you've been doing right. What kind of hobbies promote your security? What kinds of friendships keep your avoidant tendencies at bay and kindle an intense desire for bonding emotionally with other people? Your lifestyle, the food you eat, the activities you engage in, the people you hang out with, the places you visit, and even the thoughts you choose to entertain – all of this affects how steadily you'll keep on acting in a secure-attached manner.

All you have to do now is be mindful of your current behavior and how it differs from your past behaviors. A little dose of mindfulness will:

- Help you understand the correlation between your actions and emotions so you will avoid activities that promoted avoidant tendencies in the past.

- Let you observe your thoughts like an open book so you can avoid harmful and stress-inducing thought patterns and embrace security throughout your current relationship.

- Allow you to boost pro-social behaviors that are linked with emotional maturity and a deep desire to help others (Luberto et al., 2018); these behaviors reinforce security in a person's every single act of public dealing.

So, monitor your behavior as you communicate with friends, engage with your partner, and carry on with your normal life. Participate in activities that support your health – both physical and emotional.

But how do you face challenges and deal with relapse? In the next section, you'll learn how to apply resilience in different situations. Use the key skills explored in the next section to maintain your newfound security and avoid the recurring of your avoidant tendencies.

How to Stay Strong When Dealing with Challenges?

I always tell my clients to be resilient when faced with challenges and a lot of them come up with the same question: "How to be resilient? What do you mean by resilience?" Resilience has many definitions, such as:

- The capacity to bounce back from a misfortune.

- The ability to recover quickly from adverse situations.

- The motivation to go through change and adapt to new circumstances.

But my favorite definition is this: Resilience is a person's capacity to "successfully adapt to change, resist the negative impact of stressors, and avoid the occurrence of significant dysfunctions. (Babić et al., 2020)" In simple words, it is your ability to recover from any major or minor difficulty; the way you adapt to change determines how resilient you are.

However, I refuse to treat resilience as some of an innate ability. In my line of work, we do not believe that some people are brave or cowardly, strong or weak, strong-willed, or folks of weak resolve. People are either very resilient or less resilient. A resilient person is:

- A person of great willpower.

- Emotionally strong and well-endowed.

- A courageous, gutsy person.

But resilience isn't something you are born with; you develop the trait over time. It can be learned and, once learned, become a key player in your ongoing journey to maintain a securely attached romantic lifestyle. But developing resilience isn't a quest you should undertake alone. If you wish to face every setback with courage and determination, then learn to build resilience via:

- Relying on your support system to always have your back, the least they can do is tell you when you start showing symptoms of avoidance again.

- Hone your problem-solving skills so you can take on every challenge with 100% confidence and be strong in the face of adversity.

- Never let your emotions get the best of you. A resilient person is very good at the art of emotional attunement.

Still confused about how to practice resilience in real life? Check this example:

- Take deep breaths when you're faced with a difficulty instead of panicking. For instance, imagine you're slowly losing trust in your partner or feeling like they're trying to control you. Don't allow your emotions to dictate your next action; take a few deep breaths and tell yourself, "It's all under control."

- Then, reach out to a mutual friend or someone you trust. Tell that person what they think. Maybe you're being overtly suspicious, and your pal can add a neutral perspective to the whole situation.

- Talk to your friends and prepare for the possibility that your suspicions are true. Be brave and ready to move on if necessary.

- Be prepared to forgive your partner when you realize that your fears are unfounded.

Cognitive Reframing

Cognitive reframing is one of my favorite exercises. It's a fantastic way to change the way you are thinking and alter the entire narrative around setbacks. Here is how it goes:

- Take an inventory of your thoughts.

- Determine which thoughts need to go.

- Recognize the emotions connected to these thoughts.

- Ask yourself, "What's the actual purpose behind these thoughts? What are these thoughts trying to achieve?"

- Find new ways to achieve that purpose via a different thought pattern (possibly via a positive or neutral thought pattern).

- Voila! You've successfully replaced your negative emotions with positive ones.

This simple practice will help you deal with setbacks. Also, you have to lower your stress levels. Reduced stress levels are associated with better emotional resilience; a regular workout routine is associated with lower stress levels (Childs et al., 2014). You can overcome your stress and become mentally relaxed by staying physically active.

Pick hobbies that keep you on your toes, such as gardening, jogging, mountain biking, even dancing, judo lessons, or other exercises.

Resilience Building

However, there are other ways to build resilience. In simple words, "resilience" as a concept means being tough – mentally and emotionally – tough enough to navigate life and its many unique challenges with ease.

Do you want to grow tougher mentally and become strong-willed? This is what you should do:

- **Reflect on Your Past:** Think about the challenges you dealt with in the past. Ask yourself how to overcome those challenges. What worked well? How could you have responded to recurring avoidant tendencies before?

- **Be Thankful:** Assume a grateful attitude and always remember what you are grateful for in your life. Your partner, your family, an excellent job, a nice house, or something else that can help shift your focus from negative to positive.

- **Keep a Positive Perspective:** Always maintain a positive outlook on life. You must focus on things you can control and remember that setbacks are always temporary. Keep telling yourself, "These bad times will pass, and soon, I'll become a securely attached person."

- **Keep a Resilience Diary:** Write it all down – your daily challenges, how you overcome them, and what you learn from these experiences. Looking back, it will motivate you to work harder on maintaining your secure attachment style. It is a great way to remind yourself of your achievements throughout our journey together.

Create a contingency plan in case your resolve grows weak, and the power of stress compels you to go back to your old ways. This future planning involves keeping a solid support system at hand, people you can call whenever you're feeling down.

In the end, your family and friends are the ones who come to your help. You will have to rely on your support system to prevent future

setbacks. I know I've talked about creating a support system before. In the next section, you will learn how to do it right.

The Role of a Strong Support System in Attachment Theory

Let's talk about your "support system" in detail. I'm sure you have a rough idea of what it means. A support system is made of "facilities and people who interact and remain in informal communication for mutual assistance." In short, these are the individuals, people, professionals, or institutions that offer you the emotional support needed to live a particular lifestyle. In the context of our discussion, a support system will help you live a securely attached lifestyle.

Remember what I said about not taking this route alone? You don't have to be a lone wolf going your separate way. Your quest from avoidance to security must be a joint effort – at least between you and your partner.

Studies show that having a strong social support system will lower your stress levels and allow you to maintain your newfound secure attachment style for a long time (Acoba, 2024). Studies show that folks with secure attachment were less prone to psychological distress when living in isolation (such as COVID-caused lockdowns) than people with avoidant tendencies (Adar et al., 2022).

I hope you realize why having a strong support system is essential to maintain your newfound attachment and ward off the inklings of stress.

Support systems come in many shapes and sizes, including but not limited to:

- Your partner (the foundation of your support system).

- Your family members (parents, siblings, kids, or extended relatives).

- Your friends (the ones you know will always be there for you).

- Community groups (online or in-person support groups).

- Professionals (such as counselors like me and other qualified therapists).

However, you need a robust support system, a mixture of at least three from the many examples mentioned above. Regarding the last one, you should keep in mind that mental health counselors and psychologists come in many shapes and sizes as well.

Just ensure your preferred counselor/therapist specializes in Attachment Theory and realizes the weight of your struggles. Finding the right person to be your professional guide can be difficult. So, let me share some trade secrets with you:

- Do some research and collect the names of certified professionals in your locality.

- See if they specialize in treating people with avoidant tendencies and understand the challenges of this attachment style.

- Don't just check their experience or credentials, but also check online reviews and testimonials to ensure you're working with credible therapists.

- Ask for recommendations from your family and friends. They may know someone who can help you maintain your newfound security for good.

- Tell your therapy goals to the counselor so they understand what you wish to get from your sessions together and tailor their counseling style as per your needs.

These simple will help you find a good fit and get in touch with the perfect support group. If you want to maintain your security over a long period, you need to meet people who share your struggles and understand what you've gone through.

Find a platform where you can meet like-minded individuals and talk to people suffering the same problem as you are. But these platforms don't always have to be in-person. You can find plenty of online support groups as well.

- **In-Person Support:** You'll meet folks with avoidant tendencies or struggling to maintain their newfound security. A guest speaker may show up from time to time. Group discussions help attendants explore the depths of their avoidant behaviors.

- **Online Support:** You may join a chat room or an online forum to talk to people who are going through avoidant attachments. Some virtual support groups communicate via virtual calls as well.

A robust support system, therefore, is the key to maintaining your security. These online or in-person support groups will give you a sense of community. This is what you get by contacting a support group:

- You feel like you belong somewhere.

- You'll find opportunities for growth.

- You can share your stories without the fear of judgment.

- You get validated and encouraged.

- You may gain new perspectives on your experiences.

Don't think for a second that you're alone; you always have someone by your side who will help maintain your security and avoid relapse.

Hopefully, now you understand the different types of support available to you such as therapy, support groups, and others. But you must focus on building a personal support network. This support system should be a vital part of your Relapse Prevention Plan.

Relapse Prevention Plan: The Key to Maintaining Your Security

What happens when you feel inclined to go back to your old patterns and start acting avoidantly again? For that, you have to recognize the telltale signs of potential relapse. Maybe you won't notice the recurrence of these behaviors that easily.

So, here is a straightforward breakdown of some common indicators that you may be losing your grip on your newfound security:

- **Social Withdrawal:** Are you trying to avoid social interactions again? Do you try not to attend social events? Noticing a pullback from social activities? It may be a sign that you're reverting to your old patterns.

- **Rejection Sensitivity:** Do you feel fearful of getting rejected or being criticized once again? Do you tend to react defensively or withdraw emotionally to avoid getting hurt? Being too sensitive to rejection may be a sign of relapse.

- **Avoiding Intimacy:** We worked a lot to make you relaxed with the warmth of touch. So, are you avoiding physical affection and trying to maintain a surface-level connection with your partner? It may indicate you're relapsing.

- **Emotional Numbness:** Do you feel emotionally numb or disconnected? What are your motivation levels? Do you not enjoy activities you previously found a lot of pleasure in? This emotional numbness indicates relapse.

- **Escapist Tendencies:** Do you use social media excessively, binge-watch shows, take an unhealthy amount of "me time," play video games excessively, or overeat? These escapist tendencies may indicate that you're having trouble maintaining your newfound security.

But how do you counteract these early signs of relapse? It can be a bit difficult to nullify the effect of these signs. You need to address the underlying issues – the root cause of why your mind is pulling back toward avoidant tendencies. Here are some proactive steps to developing healthier coping mechanisms and nip the offshoots of your avoidant style in the bud:

- Realize that your avoidant behaviors may still be lurking somewhere in the dark entrails of your subconscious. The remnants of this avoidant attachment style can take at least a few months to disappear completely.

- Don't let negative thoughts bring you down. Refer to the cognitive reframing tip explored. It'll help you replace negative, discouraging thoughts with bright, encouraging ones.

- Stay away from situations (or people) that awaken your avoidant tendencies. It'd help a lot if you start recognizing the situations, places, or activities that trigger your slumbering avoidance. Staying away from these situations is a surefire way to avoid relapse.

Practice self-care to maintain baseline emotional stability. Self-care involves the following simple rituals:

- Get enough sleep (seven to nine hours every night).

- Drink plenty of water.

- Avoid a sedentary lifestyle.

- Perform meditation and mindfulness to ground yourself.

- Socialize with your loved ones and leverage your support system.

Once again, you shouldn't neglect the importance of a strong support network in this journey. Your partner, loved ones, friends, therapists, and others play a very important role in keeping you on track. They keep you accountable and encourage you to maintain your newfound security.

Most importantly: create a Relapse Prevention Plan tailored to your unique needs and situations. Your loved ones can help you make such a plan, and then you can tweak it how you see fit.

Personalized Relapse Prevention Plan

Here is a simplified prevention plan for you to take action. It has ten steps, but, of course, you can always add more:

- **Step 1 – Identify your trigger:** Recognize the telltale signs of relapse when they show their nasty face for the very first time.

- **Step 2 – Understand avoidant behavioral patterns:** Mind your behavior and realize when you are acting the way you did before.

- **Step 3 – Create effective coping strategies:** Find the most effective exercises (e.g., mindfulness, deep breathing, or yoga) you can use to cope with the chances of relapse.

- **Step 4 – Create a support system:** Strengthen your support system by excluding people you can't trust or who are no longer available to you for emotional support.

- **Step 5 – Set realistic goals:** Set both short-term and long-term goals to keep yourself from going back to the old patterns. For example, your goal is to attend every social event you're invited to or say "I love you" to your partner every night for a whole week.

- **Step 6 – Take good care of yourself:** Practice self-care, which will significantly reduce the chances of a relapse.

- **Step 7 – Learn how to be more assertive:** Assert yourself by clearly communicating your needs, wants, and desires. Set boundaries with other people and draw the line as politely as possible.

- **Step 8 – Remember how it affects others:** Don't forget that your relapse affects your loved ones, especially your significant other. Whenever you're about to act avoidantly, picture how your partner will feel about it.

- **Step 9 – Keep track of your progress:** Track your goals and monitor your progress. Once again, I'd like to remind you to keep a journal in which you narrate your quest from avoidant to secure attachment.

- **Step 10 – Celebrate small winnings:** Celebrate your commitment to secure attachment.

Don't forget that relapse prevention is an ongoing process, a part of the whole journey. So, keep reviewing and updating your plan as time goes by. Check in with your support groups regularly to stay on track, and soon your avoidant tendencies will become a long-forgotten memory.

Next, we'll move closer to ending our journey together. I'll share some tips with you on how to create a follow-up plan.

What's Next? Crafting a Follow-Up Plan

Do you remember the Germany Kent quote I shared at the beginning of the chapter? When you start taking note of the things you're thankful for, you lose sight of your flaws and weaknesses.

Gratefulness is just a part of the framework we'll discuss here. A follow-up plan does the following for you:

- Consolidating the changes you've achieved.
- Integrating these new habits sustainably.
- Keep a healthy mindset moving forward.
- Avoid the recurrence of your avoidance.
- Make this transformation permanent.

So, how do you come up with this plan? How do you make your newfound security a lasting change? A follow-up plan consists of these simple strategies. I have created a list of strategies for you to utilize. Grab your journal or note-taking app and write your thoughts and opinions. Think of it like a small homework at the end of this exciting adventure.

1. **Self-Reflection:** Reflect on your journey. Ask yourself how

much you've changed since you started reading this book. Can you spot any lingering avoidant behaviors? Do you still need help from a professional, or can you continue on your own from now on?

2. **Goal-Setting:** Set SMART goals to maintain your newfound security. Write down your goals. You can aim to improve your communication skills or build deeper connections with people.

3. **Develop Action Steps:** How do you plan to achieve your goals? For instance, you may attend more social events. Hang out with friends more often. Cuddle more with your loved one. Write down these action plans.

4. **Review Your Progress:** Write down which strategies have worked well for you. Which strategies have been the most effective?

5. **Maintaining Security:** Write down different ways to maintain your secure attachment style. For example, you can write which healthy activities you engage in to be in a healthy romantic relationship.

6. **Celebrate Achievements:** Don't forget to pat yourself on the back a few times. You should write down your winnings (the milestones you have achieved).

We've now moved on to the final part of our journey together. I feel it's only appropriate to end this chapter with a small section on self-care. Stay strong, stay secure, and don't let anyone bring your hopes down. Change is possible!

How to Take Care of Yourself?

Self-care makes you more resilient in the face of challenges (Martinez et al., 2021). I like to describe self-care as the foundation upon which you build the home of emotional as well as relational well-being.

Unless you're in the best of your health – both mentally and physically – you can't maintain your newfound security successfully.

Don't think of self-care as an indulgence; it's a necessity. Do you want to reinforce the key changes you've made in your personal growth journey? Then, practice self-care. In fact, self-care is a multi-faceted journey that tackles your:

- Mental health, you will notice reduced anxiety and depression.

- Physical health keeps you healthy and disease-free.

- Behavioral health allows you to avoid bad habits and behaviors.

- Emotional health keeps your emotions and feelings in check.

- Spiritual health gives you a sense of calmness and makes you feel connected to the universe.

I briefly discussed some self-care exercises previously in this chapter. Whether it's pre-scheduled quiet time, finding new hobbies, meditating, or routine physical exercises, all these activities can be part of your self-care routine. However, don't forget that self-care needs to be part of your everyday life as well.

When you're at work, home, or any other place, make self-care a priority – regardless of time constraints or lifestyle choices. This is what you can do:

- Start small. Incorporate brief, easily manageable activities into your life, such as taking a walk during a lunch break or practicing five minutes of deep breathing exercises before starting work.

- Spend pre-scheduled self-care time. You can set aside a period in the morning during your lunch break or before bedtime. Use this time to meditate or be with your own thoughts (positive ones, I hope).

- Multitasking can be a great way to make self-care part of your daily routine. For instance, I like listening to music when doing household chores.

- Say no to activities that make you uncomfortable.

- Excessive limit screen ruins your health and lead to sleepless nights (Nakshine et al., 2022). So, don't use blue-light-emitting devices (your tablet or phone) right before bedtime. Less screen time is good for your mental health.

- A sedentary lifestyle will only bring back your avoidant tendencies. You should try to make physical activity part of your everyday lifestyle. Whether you're doing yoga, dancing to your favorite tunes, or taking a short walk – find excuses to move your body.

These simple tips will set you on the path of a lifelong transformation. You can maintain your newfound security only if you're taking great care of yourself. Your focus should be boosting the mind-body connection. It's the surefire way to keep acting securely attached and stay out of the dark valleys of avoidant attachment for good.

There you go, folks! You have successfully transitioned from your avoidant attachment style to a secure attachment pattern. Self-care tips will help you stay on track and avoid relapse. I hope you can

now navigate the pathways of security on your own. Bidding you congratulations on this transformation par excellence!

Key Takeaways

- The subtle art of setting SMART goals is specific, measurable, time-bound, etc.

- Celebrating your success (even minor achievements count!).

- Maintaining your newfound security and watching out for relapse.

- Staying strong in the face of challenges and practicing resilience.

- Engaging in exercises like cognitive reframing to replace negative thoughts with positive ones.

- Creating a Relapse Prevention Plan and building a strong support system.

- Creating a follow-up plan and taking good care of your well-being; self-care is the most crucial takeaway here.

What's Next in Conclusion?

We've come a long way. Our journey together is about to end. But I won't let you go without a final word of advice. So, here's what you'll see in the Conclusion:

- We'll reflect on the journey and discuss the key points of the five steps; you will see how these stages are all interconnected.

- We'll celebrate your transformation and discuss exactly how you are changed now.

- Looking back at our quest together, you'll see how far you've come and what sort of changes you've made in your behavior/personality.

- How do you stay committed to personal growth and explore new challenges to keep yourself motivated and securely attached?

- How do you share your experiences with others and help other folks dealing with the same issue?

You have now completed the fifth and final step of this journey.

Conclusion

The End of the Journey

> "There is only one corner of the universe you can be certain of improving, and that's your own self."
>
> Aldous Huxley

The quest is complete, and through your hard work, you've gained the tools and knowledge to build secure attachments. Be reminded that:

- You are the catalyst of this transformation.

- You control the journey, and success is in your hands.

- You can choose to either go back to your old ways or maintain your newfound security.

So, let's review what we have learned!

Let's Celebrate Your Transformation

See how much you've grown. Notice the changes in your personality – the changes you have made in your behavior. In the past five steps, you have learned to treat yourself and others better.

You don't avoid emotional connectedness anymore. You don't try to pull yourself away from romantic affiliations or friendships.

- Have your thoughts changed regarding attachment and relationships? How do you perceive romantic ties? What changes? Do you look at your love life and past relationships from a new angle?

- In what ways have you noticed yourself becoming more open to your emotions? Are you more sensitive to other people's emotions? Or do you still have trouble reading people's emotions?

- Can you identify any specific situations where you acted differently than you'd have in the past? Did your new insights into Attachment Theory make you act or think differently? Are you a more emotionally intelligent person?

- Have your senses of self-esteem and self-worth changed? Do you value yourself and your romantic liaisons in a more positive light? Do you no longer prioritize your freedom and autonomy over having a long-term partner?

- Can you think of any concrete examples of healthy boundaries you've set, shown, or respected in your relationships recently? Are you more open about setting new boundaries or refusing to engage in things that make you uncomfortable?

Looking Ahead: Eyes on the Future

Congratulations! You read the whole book and applied the tips explored in the five chapters. You have now finished all five stages and transformed into a secure, attached person. Do you feel different? Do you see visible changes in your personality? How should life look like for a person with a secure attachment? Let me paint you a pretty rainbow-colored picture here.

- You realize the roots of your avoidance and learn to overcome old wounds.

- You are the one in control of your emotions and not the other way around.

- You overcame your fear of closeness and learned to balance your desire for emotional connectedness with a yearning for freedom.

- You're better at communicating your fears and concerns; the blazing hounds of vulnerability have turned into tame little kittens.

- After strengthening your romantic ties, you started reinforcing your friendships, familial bonds, and work relationships.

- You have embraced the warmth of touch and grown fond of intimacy; you don't hesitate to show physical affection anymore.

- You have made secure attachment part of your daily routine and embarked upon this lifelong journey, never to fall into the trap of avoidance ever again.

Let me remind you again, as I did in Chapter 5, that secure attachment isn't a milestone to achieve or a goalpost you reach. It's a constant journey, a lifelong process. Many clients I've met in my career think of personal growth as some sort of an objective, a mission that needs to be completed.

I always tell them, "That's a very counterproductive way of viewing progress." Self-improvement is like an ocean without a beach, a train with no station, and a cake that keeps re-spawning after it's been eaten. In the next section, I'll discuss how to make personal growth easy to tackle.

Final Words

As you close this book, I want you to embrace every moment in your life as an opportunity to practice secure attachment.

Take care of your well-being, go easy on yourself, and have some self-compassion. Significant changes take time to become permanent and setbacks are also a natural part of the process.

So, don't let failure discourage you from living life to the fullest. Keep in mind that every step forward – no matter how small or insignificant it may seem – is a step toward greater and better emotional well-being.

In addition, you now have a chance to go back to Chapter 1 and re-do your self-assessment. Evaluate the areas you can see clear improvements and the possible areas you think you still need to work on. This is a great way to keep on the journey of self-improvement towards a Secure Attachment Style.

As you keep walking this road toward secure attachment, may you find the strength you need! Keep the light of hope bright and vibrant in your heart.

Make love your bread and butter, and don't avoid those who love you back with sincerity!

Glossary

Affection: A gentle feeling of fondness or liking towards someone or something.

Assertiveness: The quality of being self-assured and confident without being aggressive.

Attachment: A deep and enduring emotional bond between individuals.

Autonomy: The ability to make independent decisions and act on one's own.

Avoidant Attachment: A style of attachment characterized by avoidance and dismissiveness in relationships.

Controlled Exposure: Gradual and controlled exposure to feared situations or stimuli to reduce anxiety.

Cognitive Reframing: A technique to change negative thought patterns into positive ones.

Cognitive Restructuring: see Cognitive Reframing.

Connectedness: The feeling of being connected or in tune with others emotionally.

Cortisol: A hormone released in response to stress and helps regulate metabolism and immune response.

Emotional Attunement: The ability to understand and respond to the emotions of others.

Emotional Pairing: Associating positive emotions with specific stimuli or experiences.

Emotional Awareness: Being conscious and understanding of one's own emotions and those of others.

Emotional Pacing: Regulating the intensity and timing of emotional expression.

Endorphins: Neurotransmitters that act as natural painkillers and mood elevators.

Focused Breathing: A technique involving mindful and intentional breathing to reduce stress and increase focus.

Guided Visualization: A relaxation technique that involves imagining positive and calming scenarios.

Intimacy: Close familiarity or closeness between individuals, often involving emotional and physical connection.

Interdependence: Mutual reliance and support between individuals or groups.

Introvert: A person who tends to be more reserved, reflective, and energized by solitude.

Extrovert: A person who is outgoing, sociable, and energized by social interactions.

Journaling: The practice of writing down thoughts, feelings, and experiences for personal reflection.

Mindfulness: The practice of being present and aware of one's thoughts, feelings, and surroundings.

Oxytocin: A hormone associated with bonding, trust, and social connection.

Positive Affirmation: Encouraging and positive statements used to challenge negative thoughts or beliefs.

Paradox: A seemingly contradictory or absurd statement that may reveal a deeper truth.

Paranoia: Excessive or irrational distrust or suspicion of others.

Resilience: The ability to bounce back from adversity, challenges, or trauma.

Relapse: The recurrence of symptoms or behaviors after a period of improvement or recovery.

Secure Attachment: A healthy attachment style characterized by trust, security, and comfort in relationships.

Self-Discovery: The process of gaining insight into one's own identity, values, and beliefs.

SMART Goals: Specific, Measurable, Achievable, Relevant, Time-bound goals used for personal development.

Subconscious: The part of the mind that influences thoughts, feelings, and behaviors without conscious awareness.

Support System: A network of individuals who provide emotional, practical, and social support.

Therapy: Treatment or intervention aimed at improving mental health, emotional well-being, or relationships.

Trauma: Emotional or psychological distress caused by a distressing or disturbing event.

Triggers: Stimuli or situations that evoke strong emotional or psychological reactions.

Vulnerability: The state of being open to emotional or physical harm, often associated with authenticity and emotional connection.

References

Acoba EF. Social support and mental health: the mediating role of perceived stress. Front Psychol. 2024 Feb 21;15:1330720. https://doi.org/10.3389%2Ffpsyg.2024.1330720

Adar T, Davidof M, Elkana O. Social Support Mediates the Association between Attachment Style and Psychological Distress during COVID-19 in Israel. Viruses. 2022 Mar 27;14(4):693. https://doi.org/10.3390%2Fv14040693

Babić, R., Babić, M., Rastović, P., Ćurlin, M., Šimić, J., Mandić, K., & Pavlović, K. (2020). Resilience in Health and Illness. Psychiatr Danub, 32(Suppl 2), 226-232. https://pubmed.ncbi.nlm.nih.gov/32970640/

Bailey, R. R. (2017) Goal Setting and Action Planning for Health Behavior Change. Am J Lifestyle Med, 13(6), 615-618. https://doi.org/10.1177%2F1559827617729634

Childs E, de Wit H. Regular exercise is associated with emotional resilience to acute stress in healthy adults. Front Physiol. 2014 May 1;5:161. https://doi.org/10.3389%2Ffphys.2014.00161

Clarke, J. & Snyder, C. (2023). How to Build a Relationship Based on Interdependence? Very Well Mind. https://www.verywellmind.com/how-to-build-a-relationship-based-on-interdependence-4161249

Hogan, J. N., Crenshaw, A. O., Baucom, K. J. W., & Baucom, B. R. W. (2021). Time Spent Together in Intimate Relationships: Implications for Relationship Functioning. Contemp Fam Ther, 43(3), 226-233. https://doi.org/10.1007%2Fs10591-020-09562-6

Iyengar, U., Kim, S., Martinez, S., Fonagy, P., & Strathearn, L. (2014) Unresolved trauma in mothers: intergenerational effects and the role of reorganization. Front Psychol, 5, 966. https://doi.org/10.3389%2Ffpsyg.2014.00966

Jahromi, V. K., Tabatabaee, S. S., Abdar, Z. E., & Rajabi, M. (2016) Active listening: The key of successful communication in hospital managers. Electron Physician, 8(3), 2123-8. https://doi.org/10.19082%2F2123

Karantzas, G. C., Younan, R., & Pilkington, P. D. (2023). The associations between early maladaptive schemas and adult attachment styles: A meta-analysis. Clinical Psychology: Science and Practice, 30(1), 1-20. https://psycnet.apa.org/doi/10.1037/cps0000108

Khoury, B., Manova, V., Adel, L., Dumas, G., Lifshitz, M., Vergara, R. C., Sekhon, H., & Rej, S. (2023). Tri-process model of interpersonal mindfulness: theoretical framework and study protocol. Front Psychol, 14, 1130959. https://doi.org/10.3389%2Ffpsyg.2023.1130959

Kogan, L. R. &Bussolari, C. (2021) Exploring the Potential Impact of a Virtual Body Scan Meditation Exercise Conducted With Pet Dogs on Recipients and Facilitators. Front Psychol, 12, 698075. https://doi.org/10.3389%2Ffpsyg.2021.698075

Kozubal, M., Szuster, A., &Wielgopolan, A. (2023). Emotional regulation strategies in daily life: the intensity of emotions and regulation choice. Front Psychol, 14, 1218694. https://doi.org/10.3389%2Ffpsyg.2023.1218694

Krishnakumar, D., Hamblin, M. R., & Lakshmanan, S. (2015). Meditation and Yoga can Modulate Brain Mechanisms that affect Behavior and Anxiety-A Modern Scientific Perspective. Anc Sci, 2(1), 13-19. https://doi.org/10.14259%2Fas.v2i1.171

Lampe, L., & Malhi, G. S. (2018) Avoidant personality disorder: current insights. Psychol Res Behav Manag, 11, 55-66. https://doi.org/10.2147%2FPRBM.S121073

Luberto, C. M., Shinday, N., Song, R., Philpotts, L. L., Park, E. R., Fricchione, G. L., & Yeh, G. Y. (2018). A Systematic Review and Meta-analysis of the Effects of Meditation on Empathy, Compassion, and Prosocial Behaviors. Mindfulness (N Y), 9(3), 708-724. https://doi.org/10.1007%2Fs12671-017-0841-8

Martínez, N., Connelly, C. D., Pérez, A., & Calero, P. (2021). Self-care: A concept analysis. Int J Nurs Sci, 8(4), 418-425. https://doi.org/10.1016%2Fj.ijnss.2021.08.007

Mohammadi, K., Samavi, A., &Ghazavi, Z. (2016) The Relationship Between Attachment Styles and Lifestyle With Marital Satisfaction. Iran Red Crescent Med J, 18(4), e23839. https://doi.org/10.5812%2Fircmj.23839

Momeni, K., Amani, R., Janjani, P., Majzoobi, M. R., Forstmeier, S., & Nosrati, P. (2022.) Attachment styles and happiness in the elderly: the mediating role of reminiscence styles. BMC Geriatr, 22(1), 349. https://doi.org/10.1186/s12877-022-03053-z

Monti, J. D. & Rudolph, K. D. (2014) Emotional awareness as a pathway linking adult attachment to subsequent depression. J Couns Psychol, 61(3), 374-82. https://doi.org/10.1037%2Fcou0000016

Mueser, K. T., Gottlieb, J. D., Xie, H., Lu, W., Yanos, P. T., Rosenberg, S. D., Silverstein, S. M., Duva, S. M., Minsky, S., Wolfe, R. S., & McHugo,

G. J. (2015). Evaluation of cognitive restructuring for post-traumatic stress disorder in people with severe mental illness. Br J Psychiatry, 206(6), 501-8. https://www.ncbi.nlm.nih.gov/pmc/articles/PMC4450219/

Murray, C. V., Jacobs, J. I., Rock, A. J.,& Clark, G. I. (2021) Attachment style, thought suppression, self-compassion and depression: Testing a serial mediation model. PLoS One, 16(1), e0245056.https://doi.org/10.1371%2Fjournal.pone.0245056

Nakshine, V. S., Thute, P., Khatib, M. N., & Sarkar, B. (2022). Increased Screen Time as a Cause of Declining Physical, Psychological Health, and Sleep Patterns: A Literary Review. Cureus, 14(10), e30051. https://doi.org/10.7759%2Fcureus.30051

Ocklenburg, S. & Frye, D. (2023). How Many Children Are Securely Attached to Their Parents? Psychology Today. https://www.psychologytoday.com/intl/blog/the-asymmetric-brain/202306/how-many-children-are-securely-attached-to-their-parents

Oz-Soysal, F. S., Bakalım, O., Tasdelen-Karckay, A., & Ogan, S. (2024). The Association Between Autonomy Need Satisfaction and Perceived Romantic Relationship Quality: The Mediating Role of Openness. Emerging Adulthood, 12(2), 187-200. https://doi.org/10.1177/21676968231220074

Reid, C. (2023, August 5). The power of celebrating small wins | Know thyself, heal thyself. Medium. https://medium.com/know-thyself-heal-thyself/the-power-of-celebrating-small-wins-and-their-positive-impact-on-life-f2fd17c3dc51

Riggio, G., Gazzano, A., Zsilák, B., Carlone, B., &Mariti, C. (2020). Quantitative Behavioral Analysis and Qualitative Classification of Attachment Styles in Domestic Dogs: Are Dogs with a Secure and an Insecure-Avoidant Attachment Different? Animals (Basel), 11(1), 14. https://doi.org/10.3390/ani11010014

Schneider, E., Hopf, D., Aguilar-Raab, C., Scheele, D., Neubauer, A. B., Sailer, U., Hurlemann, R., Eckstein, M.,&Ditzen, B. (2023). Affectionate touch and diurnal oxytocin levels: An ecological momentary assessment study. Elife, 12, e81241. https://doi.org/10.7554%2FeLife.81241

Schumann, K., & Orehek, E. (2019). Avoidant and defensive: Adult attachment and quality of apologies. Journal of Social and Personal Relationships, 36(3), 809-833. https://doi.org/10.1177/0265407517746517

Semeraro, A., Vilella, S., & Ruffo, G. (2021). PyPlutchik: Visualising and comparing emotion-annotated corpora. PLoS One, 16(9), e0256503. https://doi.org/10.1371%2Fjournal.pone.0256503

Taibbi, R. (2014). The 5 Whys to Self Understanding. Psychology Today. https://www.psychologytoday.com/intl/blog/fixing-families/201401/the-5-whys-self-understanding

Tan, T. Y., Wachsmuth, L,& Tugade, M. M. (2022). Emotional Nuance: Examining Positive Emotional Granularity and Well-Being. Front Psychol, 13, 715966. https://doi.org/10.3389%2Ffpsyg.2022.715966

Tejada, A. H., Dunbar, R. I. M.,& Montero, M. (2020) Physical Contact and Loneliness: Being Touched Reduces Perceptions of Loneliness. Adapt Human BehavPhysiol, 6(3), 292-306. https://doi.org/10.1007%2Fs40750-020-00138-0

Thomas, P. (2016). Health is wisely sharing vulnerability. London J Prim Care (Abingdon), 8(3), 33-34. https://doi.org/10.1080%2F17571472.2016.1193590

Thompson, S., Deaner, K., & Franco, M. G. (2023). How to Help Clients Make Friends. J Health Serv Psychol, 1-9. https://doi.org/10.1007%2Fs42843-023-00085-w

Tull, M. & Block, D. B. (2020). How Journaling can Help with PTSD? Very Well Mind. https://www.verywellmind.com/how-to-use-journaling-to-cope-with-ptsd-2797594

van Lankveld, J., Dewitte, M., Verboon, P., & van Hooren, S. A. H. (2021). Associations of Intimacy, Partner Responsiveness, and Attachment-Related Emotional Needs With Sexual Desire. Front Psychol, 12, 665967. https://doi.org/10.3389%2Ffpsyg.2021.665967

van Lankveld, J., Jacobs, N., Thewissen, V., Dewitte, M.,&Verboon, P. (2018). The associations of intimacy and sexuality in daily life: Temporal dynamics and gender effects within romantic relationships. J Soc Pers Relat, 35(4), 557-576.https://doi.org/10.1177%2F0265407517743076

Wang, S. K., Feng, M., Fang, Y., Lv, L., Sun, G. L., Yang, S. L., Guo, P., Cheng, S. F., Qian, M. C., & Chen, H. X. (2023). Psychological trauma, posttraumatic stress disorder, and trauma-related depression: A mini-review. World J Psychiatry, 13(6), 331-339. https://doi.org/10.5498%2Fwjp.v13.i6.331

Wardecker, B. M., Chopik, W. J., Moors, A. C., & Edelstein, R. S. (2020). Avoidant Attachment Style. Encyclopedia of Personality and Individual Differences, 345 to 351. Cham: Springer International Publishing. https://doi.org/10.1007/978-3-319-24612-3_2015

Webb, J. & Sills, D. (2023). Why Emotional Attunement is So Important, and So Healing? Psychology Today. https://www.psychologytoday.com/intl/blog/childhood-emotional-neglect/202211/the-opposite-emotional-neglect-emotional-attunement

Weber, R., Eggenberger, L., Stosch, C., & Walther, A. (2022). Gender Differences in Attachment Anxiety and Avoidance and Their Association with Psychotherapy Use-Examining Students from a German University. Behav Sci (Basel), 12(7), 204. https://doi.org/10.3390%2Fbs12070204

Yang, F. & Oka, T. (2022). The role of mindfulness and attachment security in facilitating resilience. BMC Psychol, 10(1), 69. https://doi.org/10.1186%2Fs40359-022-00772-1

Acknowledgements

This book exists because of my partner's incredible support and patience. You've been with me through countless late nights, always encouraging and handling many revisions. Your faith in my work kept me going when things got tough. Thank you for always being there to critique and cheer on me, to listen and to support me as I wrote this book.

www.ingramcontent.com/pod-product-compliance
Lightning Source LLC
Chambersburg PA
CBHW020248010526
44107CB00002B/153